Real Wealth Creation

This is a do-it-yourself book. Stella is not trying to prove that she is Warren Buffett or George Soros, she is trying to get you to change your habits. Just like a fitness programme, successful investment performance requires not only knowledge but commitment and persistence. Stella identifies the critical factors for success.

Martin Sorrell, chief executive of WPP Group plc

I was very impressed with the simple clarity of Stella Shamoon's idea to link personal financial fitness with physical fitness and the practical, almost jargon free, nature of the advice she offers readers. She brings a fresh, humorous approach to an old problem and the book deserves to be a big hit.

Euan Baird, chairman, Schlumberger

Shamoon has written a cogent, lucid guide to investing. Investors should add her insights on identifying growth companies to their investment toolkit.

William C. Steere, Jr., chairman of the board and chief executive officer, Pfizer Inc.

This book is a MUST read. Everything I have ever wanted to know about shopping for shares, on or off the Internet, with details of all the terminology and very sound advice on making and keeping money!

Jennifer d'Abo, entrepreneur

This is sound advice on investment in property – not least because Stella Shamoon highlights the pitfalls as well as the potential profits. She is also right to stress that property is a very long term investment that requires patience and persistence.

Gerald M. Ronson, chief executive, Heron International

This reads extremely well. I also wonder whether Stella Shamoon might not, over the next fifty years, make even more money than little old Anne Scheiber did. Indeed, knowing Shamoon, she may even outlive Scheiber! In fact, considering how much money Shamoon is going to make, why did she bother writing a book? You are all very lucky she has.

Nils Taube, investment guru

Real Wealth Creation

Seven Steps to Financial Fitness and Prosperity

Stella Shamoon

ORION
BUSINESS
BOOKS

The value of financial investments (including gilts and corporate bonds), quoted company shares, unit trusts, investment trusts, oeics, Isas, insurance products and property can go down as well as up. The income from most securities can go down as well as up. When you seek advice, also ask about marketability. The shares, gilts, loan stocks, insurance products and collective trusts referred to in the text of this book are for illustrative purposes only and are not an invitation to deal in them. The book was originally written in October 1999. But market conditions change and so do tax laws and other legislation that might have an impact on your investments. Neither the publisher nor the author accepts any legal responsibility for the contents of the work, which is not a substitute for detailed professional advice. Readers should conduct their own investment activity through an appropriately authorised person.

First published in Great Britain in 1999 by
Orion Business
An imprint of The Orion Publishing Group Ltd
Orion House, 5 Upper St Martin's Lane,
London WC2H 9EA

A CIP catalogue record for this book is
available from the British Library.

ISBN 0-75282-111-3

Designed by STAZIKER JONES
Printed and bound in Great Britain by
The Bath Press, Bath.

To my father, Niazi Shamoon,
from whom I have learnt much

Contents

Acknowledgements

Investment gurus Peter Stormonth Darling and Nils Taube have given me brilliant insights into investment philosophy during our many discussions over the years. Lawyer David Brecher, veteran of multi-billion-pound commercial property deals, David Tye, chairman of Rugby Estates and property entrepreneur Martin Myers have taken time to tell me of the essential dynamics of commercial property, while Jeffrey Selwyn of Allsop Selwyn, and Tim Hinks of the Woolwich have briefed me well about the technical aspects of raising loans to buy it. My savvy friend Hayley Ringrose was painstaking in pointing out the pros and cons of owning residential property to let, while another pal, Jenny Harris, read each chapter as soon as I wrote it, and was so enthusiastic about my seven steps that she gave me the heart to plod on. I am also privileged to have the endorsement of the distinguished business people who reviewed my book and liked it, and I am grateful for their generosity in time and support. Finally I want to thank my family and all my friends for putting up with my preoccupation with this book for so long, and I also beg everyone's indulgence for I am about to start writing a second!

Prologue

Get fit

Do you want to be rich?

Of course you do, otherwise you would not be reading this book right now. Well I'm sorry to disappoint you, but there is no silver bullet to real wealth creation. However, the good news is that it is not *that* hard to make money. There is just so much you can do, starting here and now, to improve your finances, and if you get on track, you *can* realise your full wealth potential in the future. It takes self-control, self-knowledge and self-confidence to succeed, so follow me in the seven steps to real wealth creation and learn how to get started and commit yourself forever to a philosophy that will make you financially fit over the long term.

The Steps

Step 1 will show you how to condition yourself for wealth. Financial fitness is just like physical fitness: you need strength, stamina, and suppleness to reach and to maintain your maximum potential. Just as in physical fitness, if you systematically work at improving your finances you can, and you will, reach your personal financial goals.

Step 2 encourages you to write an investment plan that suits you. To be successful you must be realistic. It is as important to recognise the kind of person you are as it is to identify your financial goals and assess your current situation. Step 2 shows you how.

In Step 3 we look at the choices you have. Cut through the jungle of investment jargon and discover the options that suit you best. Steps 5 and 6 will give you the low-down on shares – what and why to buy and sell – so that you can make the most of your investments.

Step 4 shows that owning property can make you real money over the long term. For some of you, owning bricks and mortar might be more reassuring and satisfying than holding just shares.

Finally, in Step 7, we take a look at the psychology of investment. Understand why you are panicking as share prices plummet and learn to take a deep breath and remain calm and rational before selling. Selling is not always the answer.

Be your own finance director

To be your own person, the *governor*, rather than the *slave*, is a financial fantasy well worth realising. Your goal is to accumulate and to go on compounding year after year a capital sum that amounts to what I call 'drop dead money'. That is enough money to afford the luxury of doing only what you want to do in terms of work. Wealth also allows you to raise your aspirations in life generally. You can become your own finance director, and you can also be your own chief executive officer at the same time.

Not only will you draw great pleasure from management of your own finances, but as your own CEO, you will also be responsible for the game plan by which you will attain your goal – a customised strategy that suits your individual strengths and weaknesses, and accords with your needs and aspirations in terms of money. You will be far more likely to stick to a plan that you have written yourself, after you have made a proper assessment of your needs and know the basic choices. You must also believe that you can do it. Absolutely.

Optimism and confidence are self-fulfilling, which is not to say that I am leading you into a mindless pursuit of making money by whatever means. By assessing your needs you can limit the risk and maximise the rewards by focusing on a few well-chosen options that are right for you.

Follow me in learning the steps of good investor behaviour – whether practical or psychological. Your self-confidence and faith in this philosophy will grow as you take each step forward. Your success in creating real wealth depends on you staying on track for the long term – not just the next few weeks or months. It may well mean making lifestyle changes, adopting new habits and developing a new positive mindset about making money, so that it becomes second nature to you.

We all know that money matters. Yet we British tend to be furtive and embarrassed when the subject comes up. In America they talk of little else, and they don't just talk. They act. America is a deeply entrepreneurial culture, where people are up front about their hunger for real wealth, and are encouraged – and rewarded – for taking risks to achieve their aspirations. But here, and throughout much of western Europe, we need to revolutionise the way we regard real wealth accumulation.

It is *not* greedy to want money, nor, for most of us, is wealth creation a hobby – it is a necessity. At every stage of our adult lives, money, and our potential to earn it and use it wisely, will play a large part in determining our standard of living and our life choices. Wealth protects and liberates us and can raise our self-esteem, never mind enhance our lifestyle generally.

It is also wonderful to be free to treat ourselves or our friends and family and to pay for such indulgence with income derived through intelligent management of your own finances and not have to justify the expenditure to anyone. Be your own finance director, and sign off the sum of money you need for such treats – after clearing it first with the chief executive officer, who also happens to be you.

But you do not often get to be CEO or finance director without persistence and patience. You will need these qualities to become financially fit. If they are in your nature, great. If not, you will have to nurture them in order to succeed at making significant amounts of money through investment. That is where the strength, stamina and suppleness required to attain a high level of physical fitness comes back to the comparison with financial fitness. It is the ability to go that extra mile, or even two.

Without that kind of stamina and staying power you will not be able to withstand the inevitable setbacks or tolerate the risks that are inherent in wealth creation. Without the suppleness to recognise major shifts in the business environment and to change your tactics accordingly in order to capitalise on these changes, you will fail to make the maximum profit from your investments. If you lack staying power and the will to persist in your wealth creation plan through thick and thin, you ought not to buy shares, on which you can easily lose 50 per cent or more of your capital in the short term when there is a general market decline. Shares ultimately reflect the growth, or otherwise, of the earnings of the businesses in which they are a small part, so shares in excellent businesses are sure to rise in value over several years. But investing in property, or putting money into your own business is worth consideration as these ways to create wealth may well suit you better than buying shares.

We all have different qualities and limitations and in investment we should bank on the former and recognise the latter. Lack of self-confidence is a weakness that must be dealt with. It is enormously destructive because every failure will confirm a sense of incompetence and fear. Whether you think you can do it, or you think you cannot – you are right! Your confidence in your ability to master the basic steps to creating real wealth is crucial. Once you know the basics, your confidence and your aspirations will soar.

Your specific experience and knowledge as employees, consumers, parents and as men and women with hobbies, special interests and skills should give you confidence. You can bring your experience and knowledge into your investments in order to attain maximum profit, at minimum risk. But whatever investments you choose, you must accept that only shares, property or building a successful business can generate real wealth – and all three involve a degree of risk. The trick is to limit the risk and maximise the profit.

So that's the trick. At this stage of the book you have a choice. You can either jump straight ahead to Step 1 or, if you need a little more convincing, let me tell you a bit more about myself and how my experience really can help you achieve the kind of financial fitness you have previously only dreamed of.

How did I begin?

My wake up call came in late 1995 when the 'Thundering Herd', as the New York-based investment bankers Merrill Lynch are known, launched me as a successful private investor. They didn't sign me up to manage the money of rich individuals, nor did their salesmen and analysts tell me how to make money from shares. No, it was far simpler than that – they made me redundant following Merrill's takeover of Smith New Court for whom I worked. That turned out to be the making of me.

The redundancy forced me to take stock of my finances and future prospects. I had to draw up my own personal and financial 'balance sheet' in order to identify my needs and aspirations and weigh them against my prospects for future earnings. At nearly fifty years old, my expectations of another high-flying City job were lower than my oestrogen levels. I had the energy and experience to hold down a top City job but I knew my age would let me down.

As I considered my predicament it dawned on me that this was my opportunity to take control. I realised that I no longer needed to do the rounds of City boardrooms trying to sell myself. I could take charge of my future financial well-being by investing in blue chip shares with a view to growing my capital over ten years. That way I need not depend on getting another full-time job to keep me in the manner to which I intended to grow accustomed as I grew older.

My personal experience will guide you through a process of self-knowledge regarding your own personal finances, and will help you understand the various choices from which to make wise, well-informed decisions in managing your finances for maximum profit. You *can* do it – and it will make your future far more prosperous and exciting – believe me!

My story

I entered journalism as a freelance, writing for a gossip column in Paris at the now defunct *Paris Presse* after a stroke of inspired luck. It was while perched on a drag lift in Villars, Switzerland, where I had gone off for a week's skiing, that I recognised this lucky break. I had been pouring my heart out to a complete stranger – a silver-haired ski instructor called Gaby – about how I dreaded returning to London to live with my parents after a fabulous year of freedom in Paris. When he asked me what I intended to do with my life, I blurted out I wanted to be a journalist. When I heard myself say it, it was news to me, but it sounded good. Gaby informed me I had just missed *le grand journaliste*, Edgar Schneider of *Paris Presse*, and advised me to ring him in Paris and to ask him for a job.

Monsieur Schneider knew everyone worth knowing in Paris – *le Tout Paris*. He agreed to send me off on assignments (those that no-one else wanted to bother with) and to pay me for any linage that was published. The adrenaline that flowed through that newspaper office was so intoxicating. It was chaotic, with, literally, people shouting 'hold the front page!' (in French) as *Paris Presse* went through its various editions. When, with beginner's luck and not a little chutzpah, I got an exclusive telephone interview with British hotelier, then just plain Mr Charles Forte, and now Lord Forte, I too yelled 'hold the front page!' Mr Forte bought three of Paris' most prestigious hotels: it was dubbed an invasion and hotel staff marched through the streets of Paris in protest.

You will understand why after such a glamorous glimpse of journalism in Paris I was intent on sidestepping the provinces and taking a short cut to Fleet Street. Not as easy as I had hoped. One day the news editor on the *Daily Mirror* asked me whether I knew where Wigan was and said he would guarantee me a job if first I worked there for a local paper for two years. I felt humiliated because I had to confess I did not have the slightest idea where Wigan was. I duly took an awayday train trip to Wigan for a recce. But much as I admire George Orwell, I had to admit I could not have hacked it in Wigan. Having interviewed the likes of Warren Beatty, Warren to Wigan seemed a drastic move, which thanks to Mr Cobb at the *Investors' Chronicle*, I did not have to make.

I can well remember talking my way into a job with the stern-faced John Cobb. He immediately accused me of wanting to use the *Investors' Chronicle* as a stepping stone to Fleet Street, where the mass-circulation national dailies were sited, with great inky printing presses and dangerously militant printers on their premises. Mr Cobb was spot on about me of course, although I protested that he was much mistaken. Just three months after joining the IC, where I wrote turgid little paragraphs commenting on company news, I talked myself into a job with the legendary Kenneth Fleet, City Editor of the *Daily Telegraph*.

The *Telegraph*'s City office was on the top floor of Bracken House in Queen Victoria Street, a stone's throw from St Paul's Cathedral. Bracken House was where the *Financial Times* was written and published. It was there that for almost eight happy years I learnt my craft and wrote about such financial fiascos as the saga of Robert Maxwell of Pergamon Press versus Saul Steinberg of Leasco. In late 1976, I left the *Daily Telegraph* for a pregnant pause, and six months after the birth of my daughter Dahlia, I joined Allied Breweries (now Allied Domecq) as Head of Press and Public Relations.

When I announced in 1978 that I was expecting a second child, I was offered a redundancy cheque, and I was very pleased to take it. Allied was hardly cutting edge about communications with the press and its shareholders, and I also really missed the independence of journalism.

After Benjamin was born I talked myself into staying at home with my two tots until they reached nursery school age. But I was kidding myself. I drove my children mad with a rigid, highly charged routine of meals and naps, interspersed with dance and gym classes for toddlers, brisk walks in the park and visits to friends who were similarly confined by motherhood. It was no doubt with relief that my two saw me go back to work early in 1982 at the *Sunday Telegraph*, where my best work was investigative, reporting on the DeLorean scandal.

In 1985, I moved to the *Observer* where the then City Editor Melvyn Marckus encouraged me to report regularly from New York on Wall Street. I built a powerful network of contacts among investment bankers, takeover lawyers and principals such as the late Lord White of Hanson. I wrote about leveraged takeover bids, financed with 'junk' bonds, and the rise and fall of insider trader Ivan Boesky. I had made a speciality of securities markets, reporting on the mergers that heralded 'Big Bang' in the City in 1986, and the October 1987 crash in world share markets. I was Foreign Business Editor of the *Observer* when sadly, I was made redundant in 1992 as the paper's then owner, Lonrho, tried to boost its failing fortunes by cutting costs. It was in the middle of a savage recession. All the 'quality' Sunday newspapers were feeling the pinch.

It was time to quit the business and to start my own – in corporate event planning. My idea was to capitalise on my contacts in the investment banking community to provide excellent services in client and executive entertainment. My company was called Touriffic Limited and it specialised in 4–6 hour themed tours for top executives, valued clients and their spouses. It was a good living and the parties were fun, but the work behind the scenes was back-breaking and not particularly stimulating.

By 1994, I had gravitated back towards financial public relations consultancy, which for me was like falling off a log, and very well paid. Then in February 1995, I joined Smith New Court on a full-time basis. That was when everything I had done in my career to date came together. I had watched and written about every aspect of what influences the financial community's appraisal of ordinary shares. The financial community determines the price of ordinary shares in daily trading on stock markets all over the world. If there are more buyers than sellers, the price of shares goes up, and if sellers dominate the day's trading, shares go down.

But experience as a seasoned journalist has taught me that the market is not always efficient when evaluating future prospects of companies whose shares are traded on the stock market. Share prices only reflect the financial community's current appraisals. Amid the deluge of data each day, the market often does not see the wood from the trees. Short-term market movements are random and often irrational. In these circumstances, long-term investors are at a distinct advantage. They can afford to ignore short-term appraisals and to put their capital into enterprises with promising future growth. This revolutionary thought – that private investors will profit over the long term by ignoring the advice industry now – is the kernel of my investment strategy.

Now, as an investor, I keep my eye only on the long-term perspective. So began my learning/earning curve as a private investor. Up until I had started to invest my own money, I had believed, like many, that successful investment required substantial sums of money, great skill, and detailed knowledge. It does not. Investment is an art. Enthusiastic amateurs do it better. In my professional life I had met only fund managers, who were not essentially interested in private investors – they were advisers for institutions. In my personal life and through my family connections, I knew only gamblers and brilliant entrepreneurs.

My parents are emigrants, Sephardi Jews who fled Iraq after the creation of Israel in 1948. After a year in Teheran we moved to London, to a Victorian mansion block in Kensington. My father, who had been an agent for BP and had a small string of petrol stations in Baghdad, exuded confidence and energy. He would get hold of lists of prime London property to be auctioned that day, hail a cab, give the driver a fat tip and ask him to drive to the sites which he, the driver, thought were of the best quality, and the most central and convenient. He would then go to the auction and bid for those sites which he and the cabbie liked.

My father worked hard and, together with his partner, built a successful hotel and property investment business. He was brilliantly entrepreneurial and allowed his instincts to guide him in business. He was my greatest inspiration and role model. He ran his business conservatively but with panache and entrepreneurial flair. But a close friend, who was just as prudent as my father at running his own business, was reckless when investing. He borrowed the funds to buy shares in a rising market and suffered big losses when the stock market crashed in 1974 and his bank sold his shares to cover his loan. I learnt that while it may be valid to borrow to expand a business over which you have control, it is crazy to borrow to buy shares, the value of which you cannot control.

What was surprising to me after I had got into share buying was how easy it was to take sensible decisions once I had defined my need as capital growth and worked out how long I had to satisfy that need. We are not talking about gambling here, but cold calculation based on rational expectations, within a realistic time frame. Even an average 10 per cent total return per year – that is dividends and share price appreciation – will double your money in just over seven years if you stay invested and plough the dividends back into more shares. That is an exciting prospect when in the workplace structural changes threaten full employment and cosy final salary pension schemes for virtually everyone.

That performance target is good enough for me, and would be for any of you who are in the cusp of your earning power and can tuck money away for several years. Mine is a conservative plan that will also work for anyone with savings which they could put out to work, while they stay at home and relish a lifestyle and standard of living which only high earners can afford, but few have the time to enjoy. I have bought shares in great companies that have infinitely better prospects than I do. While most of my savings are in shares, each individual's needs are unique, and the right mix may be different for you than for me. But how to choose the right mix of investments is what you can learn to do.

Let my story encourage you, and this book guide you to becoming financially fit and strong. I was not always like this. Like many of you I was too busy working, raising a young family and having a good time to focus on my future finances.

Managing my own finances has proved more than merely financially rewarding; it imposes self-discipline that has given me confidence and greater wisdom. I have always been persistent, but also acutely impatient. I have learnt – at considerable cost – to be more patient and less impulsive through my investments.

At first, I experienced a buying panic and purchased, helter-skelter, a vast variety of shares. I made easy-come capital gains here and easy-go losses there. But after more pain than gain, I got myself under control, and in control, through the development of a clearly defined strategy. My strategy has helped me to increase my capital substantially in just four years, even after violent volatility, and I should double up within the five years as planned.

How have I done it? It is simpler to tell you what I did not do. I did not expect a bell to toll when it was time to buy or to sell. Nor did I look to broker research for a nice little list of businesses whose shares I should buy. Broker research provides factual background and a snapshot of current appraisals of a company, sector or market. But it is largely irrelevant for long term investors like you and me. During my time at Smith New Court I saw how shares are priced and marketed, but not necessarily correctly valued.

Nor did I look to newspapers for definitive guidance on what shares to buy and which to sell. I only had to recall the ghastly atmosphere some late nights on the paper, when deadlines were upon us, and the pressure to fill the news pages distorted judgement – just like the heat crinkled the edges of the egg sandwiches that were late supper and early breakfast to us – to discount investment implications in speculative newspaper stories.

City Editors and financial pundits also continually attempt to 'forecast' when the stock market will fall. Such forecasters should be ignored. They are only guessing and might deflect you from your long term objectives. If readers are persuaded to sell on such speculative warnings of a possible general market decline, and the market either falls or continues to rise, who will tell them when to buy back their shares? Probably no-one.

Nor are the pundits likely to tell you when and what *not* to sell. Yet the premature sale of shares in a great growth company will do more damage to your future wealth than any other investment mistake. That is because you would throw out the opportunity to make future profits far greater than from cash, bonds or an average equity investment. I speak as one who sold IBM at $69 a share when, one winter afternoon, I got jittery as I watched the US technology sector go into free fall on my television screen. IBM's shares closed lower than $69 on the day, but that was cold comfort as 'Big Blue', the computer, went on to beat some Russian genius at chess and then IBM almost doubled in price (although not directly because of the chess!) over the following nine months.

I have also learnt to ignore the advice of professional fund managers. To follow them into an investment trend ('the trend is your friend' is the professionals' mantra) would often prompt buying shares because they have gone up and selling shares after they have gone down – the very opposite of sensible business practice.

For example, during the early summer of 1995, not a few professionals argued that shares on Wall Street were expensive – while those quoted on the South East Asian markets, notably on the Tokyo stock market, were better value. It was not hard to understand why American shares had gone up and Japanese shares had not.

The US economy was thriving but that of Japan was in deep recession. So I ignored the professionals' view, and piled into great American blue chip companies such Gillette, AIG, Donaldson Lufkin & Jenrette, Pfizer in pharmaceuticals, Merrill Lynch and General Motors, and relied on their marketing skills and internal strategists to decide in which world markets to invest my money.

At first my foray into Wall Street was as simple as stepping into the lift of a Manhattan skyscraper, pressing the button for the 64th floor and feeling no anxiety or discomfort apart from a pop in my ears and mild surprise at having arrived so soon. Monthly broker statements showed unrealised gain/loss against each of my investments. The ones that worked out more than compensated for those that went wrong. Rationally, such rapid growth could not be sustained. But whenever the market hit turbulence, I clung to my strategy for protection against the clamour of speculative forecasts of a crash and siren calls from stock brokers and other pundits to 'take your profits' from shares and/or 'switch into bonds'. Yes, when the market plunged, my gut lurched. It still does. In early autumn of 1998, the stock markets of the world spiralled down so rapidly that small investors who panicked and sold would have suffered savage losses. The shrewd move was to buy aggressively from these frightened people, but how many of us can honestly say we are not influenced by fear or greed in the markets?

The simple rules in my strategy help me to resist the urge to cut and run. Knowing when to sell and when not to sell is a crucial part of long term investment success. With these rules, you will apply a systematic, rational process to decisions which might otherwise be prompted by fear and/or greed.

I would never have developed my strategy without the example and inspiration of three investors, each of whom have had conspicuous success. They are an eccentric old spinster called **Anne Scheiber**, who also happened to be an investment genius; billionaire investor **Warren Buffett** and the economist **John Maynard Keynes**. These investors could not be more different in their cultural backgrounds and life styles. Yet it cannot be mere coincidence that they have all made fortunes from buying good shares and holding them over long periods of time. Here are their stories.

Anne Scheiber

Few of you would have heard of Anne. She retired in 1944, aged fifty, after twenty-three years as the first female attorney at the Internal Revenue Service. She had a nest egg of some $25,000. She died, aged 101, in January 1995, leaving a $22 million fortune in shares of American blue chip companies.

Even during the dog days of the US stock market during the seventies, Scheiber went on re-investing dividends in blue chip growth companies such as Pepsi-Cola, various pharmaceutical enterprises, notably Schering Plough and Bristol Myers, and the movie studios of the time. She hardly ever sold a share; she bought for keeps. She also had a large portfolio in New York State municipal bonds – which were tax-free. It would not have escaped her that many very wealthy individuals, whose returns the IRS inspected, had grown rich by buying shares in the 30s and 40s and not selling, whether for tax or other reasons. Scheiber's simple formula greatly inspired me; she never looked for a quick buck.

Whether Scheiber felt younger each time she bought a share is not known. She did buy shares in some fifty blue chip companies so maybe this was a form of youth 'fix'. Concentration of her capital in a few exceptional companies might have produced even more spectacular gains than those achieved by spreading her capital over such a large number of investments.

But that is being churlish. A frail and frugal five-footer, who apparently 'weighed 100 lbs soaking wet', Scheiber's passion was stocks and shares. She chose to live simply off her modest pension in a one bedroom flat with little furniture on West 56th Street between 8th and 9th Avenue in New York City. She would go three times a week to the office of Merrill Lynch on Madison Avenue and East 57th Street to see her broker, the now retired William Fay.

He told me: 'Was she a genius? No, ma'am. She was very disciplined. Falls in the market – like in the 70s – did not faze her. She never nickled and dimed an order – she just bought at market. She hardly ever sold, because she hated to pay tax. But if something did not work out, she would sell and use the losses.' Scheiber left her fortune to Yeshiva University's Stern College for Women: she wanted to help young, underprivileged Jewish women. A savvy lady: she would not have been taxed on her generous gift.

Warren Buffett

Based in Omaha, Warren Buffett has made billions with a similar **buy-and-hold** strategy. Buffett has bought shares in world class companies with global franchises in entertainment/multimedia such as Disney, financial/brokerage services such as Salomon Brothers, and mass-produced, branded consumer products, notably Coca-Cola and Gillette. He has concentrated capital in a few extraordinary companies, which he dubs the 'inevitables' to denote his confidence in their growth over ten years or more.

The unorthodox Buffett is said to find contentment sitting in an armchair, with a 100 watt light bulb beamed on to various annual reports. He is most partial to hamburgers (he bought shares in McDonald's), salted peanuts, ice-cream and Cherry Coke. Top Wall Street fund managers are spellbound by Buffett's homespun wisdom and stunning success in investment. But few fund managers are prepared to commit the weight of capital and length of time that Buffett does to his investments. He develops a close partnership-like relationship with the managements of the businesses in which he invests. He says that the proper time during which to stay invested in great companies is 'forever'.

John Maynard Keynes

Economist **John Maynard Keynes**, in a memorandum to the Estates Committee at King's College Cambridge (of which he was Bursar) in May 1938, argues that successful investment depends on three principles:

- Careful selection of a few investments (or a few types of investment) having regard to their cheapness in their probable actual and potential intrinsic value over a period of years ahead in relation to alternative investments at the time.
- A steadfast holding of these in fairly large units through thick and thin, perhaps for several years, until either they have fulfilled their promise or it is evident they were purchased on a mistake.
- A balanced investment position, i.e. a variety of risks in spite of individual holdings being large, and if possible opposite risks (e.g. a holding of gold shares amongst other equities, since they are likely to move in opposite directions when there are general fluctuations).

You can see why I have based my investment strategy on the success of such geniuses. What they achieved is not the point – it is how they did it. At first I studied the investment philosophies of these great investors and others such as Peter Lynch, Philip A. Fisher and Benjamin Graham – who taught Buffett – as well as the theories of academics such as Professor Jeremy J. Siegel of Wharton Business school. Then I devised a strategy based on my own experience and knowledge.

My fourth and biggest inspiration was my mentor, Peter Stormonth Darling, who was chairman of investment managers Mercury Asset Management during its most dynamic growth in the 80s. It was he who more than anyone convinced me to buy and hold shares in great companies and to write about my rules for maximising returns through good investor discipline. He has patiently read my drafts, argued points to help me crystallise my thoughts on paper, and whenever the market fell, Peter would despatch to me in a postcard a three-word command 'DO NOT SELL'.

Maybe 'forever' commitment to investment in shares is an elixir of youth. Scheiber lived for over a century, Buffett is sprightly in his late sixties, and Darling clocks up almost as many air miles as a long haul pilot to attend his board meetings. Equity investment keeps you young because to be successful you must remain highly consumer aware and receptive to new trends – just like a teenager. But as a mature investor, you use consumer awareness to evaluate which innovations and which trends are likely to become commercial successes and make you money.

For my part, I have concentrated my investments mainly in a few companies that happen to fit my criteria for superior growth businesses on a global scale. I intend to hold these shares indefinitely, unless death or adverse changes in the fundamental prospects of the particular businesses do us part. You will reduce risk of failure in investment by sticking to what you know and what is right for you.

Capitalise on every aspect of your personality, interests, social life, contacts and experience, whether at work or in your personal life, to make informed judgements on which shares to buy. It helps to be nosey like me, and to ask endless questions. I ask my contacts about not just their own companies' prospects, but that of rival companies. I also ask men which razor blades they use, and why. At supermarket and pharmacy tills I probe what products are purchased and by whom as I peer into other people's baskets.

I play spot the packaged branded food and baby care products mums prefer, and which over-the-counter remedies older people buy. What my young adult children buy, or want to buy, in a whole range of consumer products and services, from designer clothes to mobile phones, cars, cosmetics, foods and unfortunately, cigarettes, is also invaluable research in deciding which shares to buy. You might be interested in electronic gadgets, computer games, or science. Turn those interests into investment. When I read glossy fashion magazines or go into designer stores, I am not shopping for style, I am shopping for shares.

Of course, when share prices move up strongly and over a long period of time, we all become investment geniuses. In a buoyant share market it is all too easy to get carried away, to lose focus on the long term goal and to incur costs and losses that deplete your principles. There are many temptations out there in the stock market which may lead you to make the wrong decisions, based on impulse and emotion.

Market volatility will affect you emotionally, which is exactly why you must have a strategy and a system of rules. This book will guide you through the process that should lead you to magnificent future profits from your share investments without taking undue risk. Of course, shares are not the only investment option, but they are the best for real wealth creation over the longer term.

That is where my rules – the dos and don'ts in share buying – help to keep you out of harm's way. You should regularly recite to yourself the mantras on when to sell and when not to. I tend to repeat them while, Greenspan-style, I lie in my bath and contemplate the 'data' on which I draw for my personal investment decisions. **Alan Greenspan**, is the brilliant chairman of the **Federal Reserve Board** in the US who during the 1990s was arguably the most powerful man in the markets, but used his powers wisely to raise or lower interest rates – and with them change investor psychology from bearish to bullish respectively.

He is said to have reached these delicate decisions on monetary policy in his bathtub after contemplation, during a long soak, of a mass of complex economic data. But it was his informed good judgement and common sense that prevailed when he pulled the plug.

Likewise, while lolling in my bath, I keep reminding myself that I have bought shares in superior growth companies such as Pfizer, SmithKline Beecham, Glaxo Wellcome, Nestlé, Marks & Spencer, Vodafone, Merrill Lynch, Bank of Scotland, Shell and Gillette, and that they are virtually all household names in branded consumer products, pharmaceuticals or financial services all over the world. So what if a general market decline wiped out some of the value of these shares now? They are shares in strong, resilient businesses. If I sold them to take a profit now I would at the same time cut off greater future profits.

I have had an enormous amount of enjoyment and success putting my investment strategy into practice – and you will too. Use your own judgement and common sense, and stick to my guidelines when you invest, and you will have more fun than perhaps is decent. For money is energy and energy is power. The more you have of either, the more you can use without depleting your reserves. Why be content merely to conserve capital rather than to grow it. Money begets money. So use it or you will lose it. A little discipline is all it takes to turn your savings to a source of energy that will power you to your financial goal. Money *can* buy you happiness, for it empowers you to realise your aspirations and ambitions.

Step 1

Condition Yourself for Wealth

There is no quick fix to financial fitness, it takes commitment, discipline and self-conditioning. But even small changes in your habits now can make a tremendous difference to your financial prospects

STEP 1

Condition Yourself for Wealth

Get motivated

If anyone had told me when I was in my twenties that at the age of fifty-two I would be running five miles a day in fifty minutes and that I would also have given up smoking, I'd have said 'impossible'.

As a young girl, I was a podge who dreaded games – the mere sight and distinctive smell of a lacrosse stick still makes me nauseous. But a sad snap of me, shapeless in a white bathing suit just after the birth of my son did it. I quit a life habit of dieting and joined a gym. I then set about conditioning my body to strenuous exercise and although it was hard at the beginning, the pay-off was and still is to feel great and enjoy food, regarding it not as the enemy, but as fuel. I learnt in the process that there is no quick fix to physical fitness. It takes a long time to attain, but also that even small changes in habits and lifestyle in the meantime make a big difference to your motivation, confidence and sense of purpose.

So it is with becoming financially fit. It will be difficult at first, but will get easier. Just by doing the small everyday things right, you will eventually make big differences that will set you on the path to your goal. As you begin to see those differences, you will become even more determined to stay on track. When you eventually reach your goal, you will see that maintaining fitness, whether physical or financial, becomes automatic, effortless and enjoyable.

Think about how you manage your finances now. You know you can do better. But maybe just like those people who wait to lose weight before joining a gym, you keep making excuses to yourself. What you perhaps do not realise is how much you can change your aspirations by adopting the right habits now. It is never too late to build wealth, although the sooner you start the better, because you will have longer to make it, and longer to enjoy it.

Again, make a comparison with physical fitness. You would not think of running in the marathon until you had had a medical check-up, quit smoking, spent a few months in a gym building up your stamina and strength and conditioning yourself gradually to run ever longer distances without strain. So it is with your financial fitness. You will need to do a few 'warm up exercises' and go through an initial induction to condition yourself to become financially fit – that is wealthy – for life.

The first part is to take a long and detailed look at your finances, prospects, and aspirations. This is the financial equivalent of standing naked in front of a full-length mirror (without sucking your tummy in) and making an objective assessment of what your advantages are, where there could be improvement and what you cannot change. In this appraisal of your financial fitness, you will take your own pulse and assess your strengths and weaknesses in precise terms before identifying your long-term financial goals and starting on your programme of wealth creation.

This first part is all very well, but you will also need to make a *commitment*. Usually, some life event shakes us out of our inertia about managing our money better. Otherwise it is all too easy to put off what seems to be the boring tasks necessary to get to grips with your personal finances. We are all under pressure to accomplish our daily tasks, and at weekends it seems silly to spend time on personal finances when family and social life are pressing. The money duly rolls in each month, tax deducted, so that what you see on the payslip or cheque gives you a false sense of security.

Your net earnings are spendable, but unless you consistently allocate between 10 and 25 per cent to investment (depending on your age and prospects) you will suspend wealth creation until it is perhaps too late to make a substantial difference. Ideally you should start in your twenties, but certainly you should begin before you are forty-five in order to transform your future prospects. There is no short cut around the reality that you have to spend less and invest more to become wealthy. Only when you have accepted that reality, and all it implies in terms of commitment, discipline and self-conditioning, will you be ready to embark upon Step 1. This strategy is not about new year resolutions to cut back and save up for a while. It is about developing new habits, instincts and reflexes that will make you financially fit.

Wealth creation, for most of us, is not an option. It is a necessity. You may be relatively financially secure now, with a job and maybe prospects for promotion. But employers cannot guarantee anyone a job for life so any security that you feel may be misplaced. You have to build financial strength and resilience into your life plan, which will enable you to withstand the inevitable shocks and setbacks and give yourself and your family far better protection than employers or the state can offer you long term.

Before we get around to assessing your current financial condition in detail, just take a piece of paper and do a quick calculation of what you think is your **net worth** *now*, that is your total assets minus your liabilities. Then write down what you would like it to be in order to feel secure and to attain financial fitness. (See page 14 for how to calculate your net worth.) The chances are the second figure is at least double the first. You want more wealth but you are focused mainly on how much more income you might derive from work in order to attain it. You are missing the point.

You are probably earning enough now to start to create real wealth over several years. But before you start, you have to really want to be wealthy and to believe it is in your power. That, just as physical fitness depends on conditioning yourself to eat less but better food and exercise more as a way of life, so wealth creation is a direct consequence of consistently spending less and investing more.

But why should you sacrifice now for future prosperity? Because by taking action now you can determine your financial destiny, become financially independent and thus protect yourself and dependants even if your earning powers wane later in life.

But why worry now, you might ask. As long as you have enough to pay for the necessities: the mortgage or rent, insurance, school fees, car and travel expenses, food, clothing, household goods, entertainment and other items in normal monthly expenditure, there seems no compelling reason to try to do any better. Most of us tell ourselves we are doing all right, maybe better than our parents and at least as well as our friends, who are just like us moneywise.

It is so nice to be among People Like Us. We share similar standards of living. It is uncomfortable to think about breaking this cosy mould, revolutionising our aspirations in the wealth stakes, and budgeting to create future wealth. Besides, we all know people who have been more successful than us and have made a lot of money. But we tell ourselves that in order to become wealthy they have had to sacrifice a great deal, or risk a lot, or else they have been plain lucky. We cling to the touching belief that 'luck' will make us millionaires – just witness the number of lottery tickets bought each week. The odds are 14 million to one against you.

Sound familiar? That was me until the monthly pay cheques stopped and I realised that I would face problems with my finances in the future unless I took drastic action immediately. Ironically, I had for years written savvy columns about business and finance, yet had a very vague grasp of my own finances. The French say: 'Le chausseur mal chaussé', which means 'cobblers are shoddily shod'. Yes, I was ever so clever yet so dumb about managing my own money that I did not even latch on to **PEPs** and **TESSAs** until late 1995.

There were many moves I should have made to invest the surplus over my normal monthly expenditure while I was employed. But I just could not be bothered to wrap my brain around the options, or make decisions that would 'tie up my capital'. So I bumbled along for years, with a dim notion that I ought to manage my money better, but not making a conscious decision to get started until I had no choice.

If I had started on a methodical and persistent investment plan when I was in the cusp of my earning power I would now be very rich, and probably have quit salaried work many years ago. But I was sloppy, partly because I was so busy and stretched. The last thing I had energy for at weekends was personal finance planning. Every now and again, I would decide to save up – note that this peculiarly British habit is a prelude to spending and therefore wholly incompatible with saving in order to invest for future wealth. For example, in 1986 when I was earning good money as a financial journalist, and my husband Joe was at an American bank, what did I do with the £11,000 I had saved up? I blew it all on a new kitchen, complete with white marble floor, pink granite work tops, Italian gadgets and – a total write-off – the services of a 'designer' whose planning was so flaky that we had no kitchen at all for weeks.

In those days Joe seemed always to be following me around with one of those fearful black ledger books, trying in vain to persuade me to write down the relevant facts about my personal finances, or at least to record my income and expenditure. Joe would badger me to budget in that wretched black book on Sunday evenings when I was bereft of adrenaline and energy, having worked late into the early hours of Saturday morning writing my features for the *Observer*. I procrastinated, and often we'd row over my inability to apply to the family finances the same discipline and energy I put into my work. Budgets to me were what chancellors delivered. I was very much in the earn-and-spend camp in those days (when, remember, I also smoked and mistook thin for fit). My money habits were good for the economy but not for me.

When, years later, I came to realise how much I could have done for myself with a simple, but systematic plan, (including logging my expenditure in a black book!) I kicked myself. Not least because once I got into it, running my own money became almost a hobby, certainly not a chore. The process becomes enjoyable, because you are motivated by the pay-off. Do not be daunted by the discipline and persistence you will need to reach your full financial potential and to create real wealth. It will become fun.

You should by now be convinced that you can apply commitment and effort to this plan, so let's make a start and begin with some practical preparation.

EXERCISE 1
Consolidate your debts

The first exercise to limber up for lifelong financial fitness is to quit the financial equivalent of smoking – credit card debts. Indeed, if you both smoke and have credit card debts, it is a no-hoper. Give up the evil weed and save some £1,300 a year if you are a one-pack-a-day addict, and £2,600 a year if you are on two packs (at 1999 prices). Nicotine patches *do* work, and they cost a mere £15 or so for a week's supply of seven. You stick a patch on the flattest part of your body every day for nine to twelve weeks to wean yourself off nicotine. The patches dispense a decreasing amount of nicotine through your skin until you are free of addiction.

I can think of no better analogy with letting debts run up on credit, which is also a form of addiction. Even if you are not lighting up, when you juggle bits of plastic to make your income last throughout the month, you are still burning money. An 'anti-debt addiction patch' would transform your life. You could cut up all your store cards and consolidate your outstanding debt into one credit card, like a nicotine patch, which offers the best deal in terms of annual charge (the best deal will be one that has no annual charge) and the lowest **annual percentage rate** (APR).

Then, over nine to twelve weeks, you could stick that single piece of new unused plastic on to a flat part of your body out of easy reach – that should stop you spending! Of course that is a bit extreme, as is the suggestion that putting your credit card in a tub of water and freezing it in the icebox is a way of weaning yourself off the credit habit. However, if you really cannot trust yourself not to use it, and believe me, many people can't, then such measures may be appropriate. Otherwise, leave it at home. Replace your credit card in your wallet or purse with a debit card (e.g. Switch). Tell yourself to pay hard cash from now onwards because your credit has been cancelled indefinitely.

Meanwhile, aim to pay off your old debt in equal parts each month while you are still enjoying a low introductory APR on your new card. If you cannot trust yourself to send in a monthly cheque, then do it by direct debit. In this way you will gradually rid yourself of your dependence on short term financial fixes and condition yourself to think before you purchase goods and services you could live without. It will be painful, but it will be worth it.

If you think life will be too miserable if you can't enrich it with credit, just think how good it will feel to read your (single) credit card statement each month and see that the total debt and finance charges have been reduced. Now recall how sick you feel now whenever you tally the shock cost of your barely memorable consumption during the previous four weeks.

Once you have paid back your old debts, you can start to use your credit card again. But you must restrict its use strictly to the convenience of settling bills in foreign currency or for large ticket items such as a washing machine – and then spend only if you have first made adequate provision for such expenditure from next month's pay. Be careful to pay back promptly or that 'free credit' will put you back into debt just as surely as a single drink can sink an alcoholic. It's a good idea to try to live without a credit card at all for a while. You will be surprised at how easy it becomes.

EXERCISE 2
Build your knowledge

The next warm-up exercise will gradually develop your knowledge and understanding of how to make money. Routinely read the weekend press, notably the *Financial Times* or the *Times* sections on personal finance. For the price of a few pence each week you will put yourself through a study course that will build up your confidence and make you aware of what new products and services are available in the market, how they compare and how they apply to your financial needs.

Keep a notebook handy to jot down any investment ideas prompted by them and/or action points to follow up, or even to make a note of any words or phrases you don't understand. Do not be afraid to ring up the various providers of financial services (usually on freefone numbers) and quiz them thoroughly about costs, terms, tax treatment, flexibility, and penalties of their products. Practice probing the purveyors rather than merely skimming the often unintelligible fine print in their prospectuses and/or buying into the sales patter of commission-hungry salesmen without fully understanding the potential risks and benefits involved. As legendary investor Warren Buffett put it, risk comes from not knowing what you are doing.

If you really do not have time to read up on personal finance over the weekend, highlight the articles that are relevant to you, keep the newspaper in your bag or briefcase and read it on the train on your way to or from work, or in your lunch hour.

EXERCISE 3
Supple up

A third warm-up exercise will build your suppleness financially. Get into the habit of checking that you are keeping your savings and getting your mortgage/fixed loans at the most competitive rates. The Money section in the Saturday edition of the *Financial Times* is an excellent guide. Of course you must still check out the facts yourself before investing, as conditions, penalties and interest rates may vary from those published. Monitor what is available, and be prepared, if necessary, to keep moving your money from one bank, building society or other to the provider that gives you the best introductory offer. They all talk glibly of 'client relationships' but what they do is 'client marketing', so that new clients get the best deals.

They will lure you for a limited time with higher than average interest rates on your savings, or if you are a borrower, lower than average APR for credit. But when your time elapses, so does their charm initiative, and rates invariably change against you. That is the time to move on to a better deal as another organisations' new client. New lenders, such as Sainsburys, the Prudential's Egg, and overseas banks unburdened by an expensive branch network have stormed UK retail banking, and are shaking up the cosy complacency of high street banks and building societies.

FT Money also runs tables of unit trusts and investments trusts, highlighting 'winners' and 'losers' and logging each within its specialisation – such as UK Growth, Global Emerging Markets, and so on. Peruse these carefully each week – it will help to increase your understanding before making investment decisions.

The run-down on markets, written with humour and without too much jargon, is a must-read to get a grip on the action of the previous week. You can ignore the technical bits not relevant to you but the *FT*'s personal finance pages, editorials and Lex column will key you into issues and events currently prevalent in the market. You will find it all readable and enjoyable after a while.

Know your vital statistics

These three simple warm-up exercises will start to attune you to some of the key factors which together can enhance – or damage – your financial health. It is also part of this induction process to make a thorough assessment of your financial state, so as to identify your financial needs and write a plan to meet your objectives. When you have completed the induction, which takes in another three rather harder exercises, you will be ready to learn what options are available to help you meet your goals, and you will be ready to tackle even more advanced exercises later.

EXERCISE 4
Complete a fact-find on your finances

For this exercise you need to use actual figures to make projections, define your needs and objectives and eventually arrive at a realistic and sustainable plan. First you must identify your free funds. For free funds, read savings after setting aside all short to medium term financial commitments such as family obligations, insurance, debt servicing, house financing/improvement, tax liabilities, and a realistic budget for monthly income and expenditure, along with an emergency fund held in an instantly accessible form. A reasonable emergency fund should amount to about three months' essential expenditure.

Section One

The first section of the fact-find should embrace personal details. In it you should note the following details:

PERSONAL DETAILS	YOURSELF	YOUR SPOUSE/PARTNER
Name		
Age		
National Insurance Number(s)		
Children's names, ages		
Any other dependants		

EMPLOYMENT DETAILS	YOURSELF	YOUR SPOUSE/PARTNER
Occupation		
Employer		
Position		
Length of service		
Remuneration		
– gross income		
– bonus/overtime/commissions		
– profit share		
– savings related share options		
– benefits in kind e.g. company car/allowance, medical cover		

You will not have all these details at your fingertips – you must find them out. You have to do your homework before you can quantify the surplus/shortfall in your earned and unearned income in the near term and plan your savings and investments sensibly to meet future obligations, such as school fees, medical provision for elderly dependants or the purchase of a second home.

Pension arrangements, whether company/employer's or private, should be precisely detailed. Few people take the time to study their pension provisions or decipher the jargon in the material provided in their pensions booklets.

Make time. Ask questions. Ensure you fully understand what your pension is projected to provide (see Step 3). Lay out all this information to look at the big picture and see how each piece fits in the jigsaw.

Your pension details must include the following facts:

PENSIONS	COMPANY PENSION	PERSONAL PENSION	STATE PENSION	AVC/FSVC
Retirement date				
Company or fund				
Regular or other contributions				
Current value				
Projected value at retirement				

If you have any pension benefits from former employers include the details in the previous table.

Section Two

The second section of the fact-find collates your financial information. This is a detailed schedule of your financial assets/liabilities (whether individually or jointly held) along with your income/expenditure.

ASSETS

USED ASSETS	£	INVESTED ASSETS	£
Your home		Stocks & shares	
Other property e.g. second home		Investment property	
Antiques, art works, vintage cars/wines		Deposit accounts	
Emergency funds (three months of essential expenditure)		Current accounts	
Totals	**A**		**B**

LIABILITIES (– = not applicable)

MORTGAGE	DETAILS	£
– Lender		–
– Type		–
– Amount outstanding	–	
– Repayment date		–
– Monthly payment	–	
– Interest rate (fixed or variable)		–
– Redemption terms		–
– Life policies to cover mortgage		–
– Are repayments covered for sickness/redundancy		–

BANK LOANS	DETAILS	£
– Lender		–
– Amount outstanding	–	
– Repayment date		–
– Monthly payment	–	
– Interest rate (APR)		–
– Redemption terms		–
– Are repayments covered for sickness/redundancy		–
CREDIT CARDS AND OTHER DEBT		
– Lender		–
– Amount outstanding	–	
– Interest rate (APR)		–
OTHER LIABILITIES - SPECIFY		
TOTAL LIABILITIES **C**	–	

NET WORTH = A+B-C

Now compile a monthly income and expenditure summary. The first part will be a net income statement. Include earned and unearned income.

GROSS INCOME	YOURSELF £	YOUR SPOUSE/PARTNER £
Earned, i.e. salary/fees/commissions		
Unearned income i.e. investment income		
State benefits such as child allowance or pension		
Totals **A**		

DEDUCTIONS	Yourself £	Your spouse/partner £
Income Tax		
National Insurance		
TOTALS **B**		

NET INCOME = A-B

Ensure that you use all available personal and other allowances and exemptions.

Now break down your *actual* expenditure into three categories in order of priority.

EXPENDITURE

MUST SPENDS	£	MIGHT SPENDS	£	MINDLESS SPENDS	£
Mortgage/rent		Savings & investments		Gambling	
Building/ life insurance		Holidays		Cigarettes	
School/ course fees		Eating out		Evening shoes	
Food & drink (at home)		Publications, television, videos, computers		Copper-plated stationery	
Council tax		Cinema, theatre, clubs		Silly new gadgets for kitchen/car	
Medical/health insurance		Entertaining at home		Slimming pills	
Basic clothing		Gardener, flowers		Debt servicing on credit cards	
Water, telephone, gas & electricity		Fashion accessories, jewellery, new clothes		Parking/ speeding fines	
House repairs		Personal care		Other general waste (be specific)	
Child care/ home help		Fitness, health			
Car expenses		Gifts, donations			
Essential travel e.g. work		Home improvement, decoration			
Other (be specific)		Art, antiques			
TOTALS					

	£
Total monthly expenditure:	
Net income	
SURPLUS/SHORTFALL	

EXERCISE 5
Reallocate expenditure to create wealth

This exercise focuses on the three categories we have just identified: mindless spends, might spends and must spends and it could prove even more difficult than all that homework in Exercise 4. You will notice that I have deliberately omitted the B-word. In order to condition yourself to spend less and invest more, budgets are not the answer. They are like strict diets. Once you come off them you feel out of control and are likely to go on a mad spending spree – probably on credit. The logging of your expenditure in the three groups over the next several weeks will enable you to get a tight grip on how you are spending your money now. Your aim will be to reallocate as much of the money you now waste from the mindless spends category to the more rewarding might spends, and then to move savings and investments from might spends to the top priority must spends category.

You can do this by reducing your expenditure in areas where you have discretion. Spend less on restaurants and clubs (notice that I say less rather than nothing), eliminate interest charges on credit cards, cut out fines for parking and speeding and stop gambling. If you are hooked on the thrill of taking risks, take calculated risks, via investments. When you get it right you will derive a life-enhancing benefit in the form of real wealth creation. Get yourself a hard-backed cashbook and start today. Note every single purchase and running expense in chronological order and allocate it to the appropriate category. You could use different coloured pens or different computer files to keep the three categories separate. Just by becoming aware in precise terms of how you are spending your money, you should automatically start to change your money habits for the better.

Think of it like this. How many of us these days are not aware of the fat/protein/carbohydrate content of foods as we eat them? We know some are nutritionally better value than others. We may still crave, and eat, junk food occasionally. But if we choose to eat food that is bad for our health, we do so knowingly, totting up the fat and calorie content as we munch, without having to refer to a nutritionist. In the same way you can reach a point where you are aware of your spending – what is necessary and what is not – without even trying.

EXERCISE 6
Stop!

This is the final exercise in this induction process. It should not be attempted until at least twelve to sixteen weeks – or indeed several months if you still feel unsure of yourself – after you have completed your fact-find and started logging your monthly expenditure. The exercise is to stop.

You should have re-educated yourself in your spending habits by this stage, and be ready to draw a line under the past. For the future, you will soon be ready to write down your financial goal and a plan to meet it. At this stage it might still seem like an impossible dream, but when you have made the commitment, conditioned yourself for wealth, and learnt the basics of wealth creation, with each step you take you will be able to return to your fact-find, look up what you originally stated as your goal and, I hope, raise your aspirations even higher. You should have gained the confidence to visualise yourself ten years from now, write your own financial history as you ideally want to be – and then *make it happen*.

From the information collected in the fact-find you should be able to quantify accurately the amount of free funds that you can allocate long term to shares and short term in deposits, either for emergencies or short to medium term obligations. You will see the weaknesses and exposures, along with the strengths, in your personal finances.

From the start of your wealth creation plan, the most critical facts to identify are what is the maximum you can afford to put into a long term equity investment portfolio, and what is the very least you need in capital safe, more short term savings such as National Savings, short term gilts, building society or bank deposits. You will understand why in a minute, when you read on to the end of Step 1.

Your home and other property are fixed assets and are therefore not part of your free funds. Fixed assets should not be used as security against which to borrow money for investment. If you buy shares with borrowed money, you surrender your unique strength – the luxury of time, and control of the timing on when or when not to sell. Do not borrow to buy shares – use only your own free funds for long term investment and stay in control of your investment plan.

The amount you tuck away in shares, whether in lump sums or via regular monthly transfers from your pay, must be realistic given your financial objectives, circumstances and the amount of time you have allowed yourself to realise these objectives.

When you buy shares, you must stay locked in through thick and thin for several years. The risk of losing capital from shares is very high in the short term. But eventually the value of shares adjusts to reflect the earnings of the businesses in which they represent a small part of the ownership.

So the essential point to grasp right now, before we get on to Step 2 is that for all the plethora of complex investment products available to you, there are only two basic ways to put your money out to work. You can use it to become an owner, by buying shares, property or a business. Or you can put your money out as a lender. It does not take Einstein to work out that as an owner of good property, or shares in first class businesses, you will, over several years, enjoy real growth in the value of your money – and thus create real wealth – whereas you would make very little if you merely lent your money short term to the bank, building society or to companies and/or governments via bonds and gilts. Even when you could get some 15 per cent on your savings in the early 1990s, your real return was paltry because **inflation** was almost as high. Learn to think in terms of real rates of returns.

For example, in the US in early 1999, you could get 5.5 per cent on the benchmark 30-year Treasury bond, while inflation was 1.5 per cent.

The real return was not 5.5 per cent, but 4 per cent – the net yield, after inflation. Savers rejoice in high rates of interest, even if high inflation erodes their real return. Investors feel bad when inflation and interest rates are low, and prices and wages are stable. They feel good when the value of their homes is rising, and pay rises pre-empt and outstrip the rate of inflation. But those responses are financially inappropriate as inflation leads to erosion of capital.

You do not need to be a genius to understand that the higher potential profits from shares, property and your own business is directly related to higher risk of loss, which you would assume as an owner. Accordingly, you cannot expect more than relatively poor returns from being a mere money lender, because you are not putting your capital on the line. All you are doing is parking it.

So to summarise Step 1:

- Make small changes in your habits and everyday routines *now* that will lead to a big difference to your wealth prospects in the *future*.
- Take the time to write a complete fact-find as part of your reconditioning.
- Log your monthly expenditure and reallocate more to investment – a top priority.
- Condition yourself to spend less and invest more for the long term.
- Accept that you cannot create wealth by merely lending out your money.
- Recognise you will create wealth only if you have the guts to be an owner.

Step 2

Write a Plan That's Right for You

We each have unique financial needs and objectives.
Assess yourself and decide what is right for you

STEP 2
Write a Plan That's Right for You

Having completed Step 1 you should now recognise that there is no quick fix for creating wealth and that you will not win at the money game unless you systematically save more and invest enough to build your future finances. You have adopted some good investor habits, such as reducing your credit card debt and reviewing your finances each week to check whether you are on the best available saving/borrowing rates, and to see what new financial products or services are on the market. You have started to condition yourself to create wealth for life by logging your expenditure into three categories in order of priority as a prelude to reallocating non-essential spending to the top priority of regular savings and investments.

Most important, during your induction, you completed a fact-find. This embraced an income and expenditure analysis and a realistic, market valuation of your liabilities juxtaposed against all your assets.

The purpose of compiling your fact-find was to establish your net worth. You can look at this fact-find to see a snapshot of your current finances. The next step is to try to imagine by how much your finances should grow in order to meet your responsibilities and aspirations over, say, five to ten years. The outline, albeit it shadowy, of your financial needs and an overall plan to satisfy those needs should start to come into view. We are not talking about a wish list here, but a plan based on conservative assumptions, designed to work within a realistic time scale.

None of us can predict the future. Such unpredictable life events as marriage, parenthood, job mobility in terms of geography and function, inheritance and, sadly, divorce, illness and redundancy will impose different strains and opportunities on us. All the same, if you fail to plan your future finances now, you are planning to fail at wealth creation.

It takes a long time to build real wealth. Your overall gameplan should embrace at least five years, but preferably ten or even fifteen, and you should review it every year, not necessarily to change it radically, but rather to take stock of what has been achieved, what mistakes you made, and to see how you might improve the overall result.

The discipline of writing a long term plan, with explicit and realistic investment objectives, will give you the confidence to stay on course. Your objectives must be based on your actual needs and they will determine the risks you must assume to achieve them. Without goals, you can only assess risk by your emotional response to it – which broadly falls into two extremes: fear and greed. You must avoid both these extremes to be a successful investor. You can, and you will, if your financial objectives are realistic and the investments you choose are appropriate to meeting those goals.

If your circumstances change in the future, you can always alter your plan accordingly and write another that is more appropriate. You may for example, reach your initial objective in less time than you predicted – in which case write a second, more ambitious plan. But always start with realistic goals in investment and work the rest out from there. Even after a bad year in the markets, your goal should still hold good and your plan still make sense, so stay on track. Just as a coach might advise an athlete to 'plan your play and play your plan', I say stick to a systematic, disciplined plan to achieve your long term financial goals.

Private investors like you and me are not like the professionals. Institutional investors are under commercial pressure to produce superior performance in the short term. We, on the other hand, have specific financial objectives, such as saving up for the deposit on a house or paying for our children's private education, or boosting our retirement fund. We must apply an investment strategy to meet those needs. Although stereotypes exist, very few of us really match them so we each have unique financial needs and objectives – there is no template that will suit us all. Certain factors will determine aspects of your unique investment plan.

They are:

- Age.
- Income/employment status.
- Risk tolerance.
- Goals/aspirations.
- Tax status now, and in 5 – 10 years.
- Time scale.
- Inflation now, and in 5 – 10 years.

Before you consider how the above might affect your long term game-plan, make sure you have first put into your wealth creation kit four basic tools so that you are not forced to sell long term investments to meet your short term needs:

1. Make sure you live in a place that you like and can comfortably afford.
2. Put at least three months of must spends on short term deposit for emergencies.
3. Take out life insurance and any other relevant protection, but only if your dependants would have to shoulder a substantial financial liability such as a mortgage in the event of your illness, disability or demise.
4. If you have not already made provision for an adequate pension or some other means of funding your retirement, make that one of the priorities in your long term plan.

Now you are ready to look at your longer term financial needs and to write a plan to satisfy them. Your age will determine how long you have to invest in order to build your wealth.

Twenty-five to thirty-five

If you are in your mid-twenties to early thirties, you should go for it. You could easily increase your capital by several times over if you stay invested and persist in regular investment in growth shares and/or investment property over the next ten to fifteen years.

Time gives you great power in investment – as long as you have allocated a realistic amount to reach your goal. The younger among you have the time to take a calm view of market volatility. You have the time to earn more by putting your money out to work for longer. The magic of compound interest over time (see Step 3, page 58) can make even a conservative annual total return of 10 per cent double your money in just over seven years (as long as you keep re-investing your income and stay invested over that time). In twenty years, a 10 per cent compound rate of return would make your money grow almost seven-fold.

So do not waste precious time by procrastinating over when to start creating wealth. At your age, in full employment, you can forgo income now and concentrate on capital growth by investing aggressively in specialist funds, and also concentrating money in a few directly held shares. But always remain within the context of your goals – and assess the risk in what you buy (and sell) according to that context.

Thirty-six to forty-five

If you are in this age group and employed, you too can afford to be aggressive in a gameplan to grow your capital over ten to fifteen years, or longer. You should concentrate virtually all your capital in growth shares where you may suffer from short term price volatility, but you will still have the time and the resilience, assuming you are now well established in a career or business, to ride out market ups and downs. Go for blue chip growth shares or perhaps buy an investment property, so that you can leverage a relatively small capital base into a large capital asset on borrowed funds – and deduct the costs from tax.

Forty-six to sixty

At this age you should still be thinking in terms of a long term plan to grow your capital, as an owner of shares or investment property or via your own business. But unless you have substantial income and can afford to adopt the high risk tolerance of someone of twenty-five (who unlike you has ample time to grow into an investment genius!) you will want to be more cautious in your expectations and the level of risk you assume to meet your goals.

The likelihood is you will be focused on boosting your retirement fund or you may want to top up your pension plan. The broad investment options are outlined in Step 3. You could choose income funds, gilts, guaranteed income bonds, or high yield shares, such as utilities, for more income and protection of your capital as you get nearer to retirement; but growth shares should also be in your portfolio. When you move on to Step 5 you will see that I recommend that you don't buy utilities, but that is for growth – they can be a wise investment at this life stage. Again choose only investments that will help you reach your goals within a given time frame. If you do not need to take higher risks to meet your objectives, why should you want to?

Over sixty

If you are over sixty years old and are still intent on growing your wealth, you have little choice but to stay invested essentially in growth shares or property and tolerate the risk of short term capital loss. You must plan your future finances so as to ensure that you can maintain your standard of living and have enough resilience (or insurance!) to be able to afford healthcare and medical expenses – which rise much faster than inflation. That implies capital growth as well as rising income. But you may want to switch a proportion of your investments from growth shares, with low yields, to higher yield, capital safe, inflation-proofed savings, such as index-linked gilts and National Savings certificates.

Work for money, but make your money work for you

Your disposable income and employment status will determine how much purchasing power you can afford to forgo now in order to invest for future wealth. If you take age and income into consideration, the younger among you, with less income with which to invest, and more financial commitments and responsibilities such as rent/mortgage repayments and a young family, may feel at a distinct disadvantage. You are at a lifestage, whether as a single, young married or young parent, when invariably you feel broke and have to work hard to keep up your financial commitments.

But while we wrinklies may be on higher incomes because we are in the cusp of our earning power, and are likely to have fewer financial burdens, as our mortgages will have been repaid and children will almost be independent, we do not have so much time to transform our future wealth prospects as do younger investors. It is not just the amount of money that is invested to create wealth that matters, but also how long money remains invested so that the growth in capital and income compounds.

Meanwhile some of those who are retired might be constrained by restricted pension income from pursuing capital profit rather than capital protection strategies. But there is no reason why those who are still rudely financially fit should not be as aggressive as twenty-five-year-olds in terms of growing wealth. They will have the financial resilience to withstand short term losses, and long experience of market fluctuations should make them psychologically strong and able to resist fear. They may be under pressure from advisers and descendants to plan tax-efficient ways to give their money away. But they should not forget King Lear!

Look what happened to him when he gave his wealth away to his daughters and relied on their generosity to maintain his standard of living. He'd have been better off dying rich and leaving his daughters a large tax bill. Yet, as they get older, so many professional and business people are brainwashed into concentrating on giving their fortune away rather than continuing to create wealth and enjoy it. Inheritance tax planning is wholly appropriate for those with more than enough wealth to see them out in style. But elderly investors with modest fortunes should not give money to their children and grandchildren just to save tax.

None of us knows how long we are going to live or how much health care we might need, and at what cost, as we reach the end of our lives. Unless we die in an accident or from some critical illness, we are likely to live for longer than may be enjoyable or affordable. Healthy elderly investors still need to stay invested to bolster both their capital and income to maintain a dignified standard of living hopefully in the quite distant future.

A more appropriate way of passing on your wealth is to bequeath shares. The lucky recipients can work out efficient tax planning, or even pay inheritance tax – they will still benefit. For elderly investors, a buy-and-hold strategy in share investment also happens to be good tax planning. On death, capital gains tax liability is cancelled. Surviving spouses have no inheritance tax or capital gains tax to pay on inheriting the portfolio of shares, although when they pass away, the wealth passed on may be liable to inheritance tax.

There is risk of loss in every type of investment – even when you do not invest, you risk loss of opportunity or loss through inflation. But some investments can be inherently riskier than others, unless you know how to use them. In Steps 5 and 6 we shall look at how to reduce unavoidable market risk when buying and selling shares, and which type of shares not to buy at all in order to eliminate avoidable risk.

Risk tolerance

Here, we consider risk tolerance. Financial advisers often talk of risk tolerance as if it were a measure of your pain threshold, which it is not. Risk tolerance should be a cold calculation of the level of risk you are prepared to accept to achieve your goals. Emotion and pain ought not to enter the equation of risk tolerance.

Risk has to be equated to your goal. Forget the perceived wisdom that the greater the risk in investment, the greater the potential reward. That implies the more risk you take, the more money you will make, which is absurd. You can always increase your risk without adding the potential for reward, by being stupid or greedy, so why do it? Indeed at market peaks, investors are willing to assume excessive risk because greed takes over from rational risk assessment.

Witness intelligent private investors chanting 'Cash is Trash'; bailing out of 'boring' blue chip shares, and putting their money into high yield Russian bonds during 1998 – the year Russia defaulted. All that was not about risk tolerance, but greed. When investors rush to sell (the cry then of course is 'Cash is King') they are not usually making rational risk assessments, but are gripped by fear. Never confuse greed with risk tolerance, or conversely, fear with risk aversion. (See Step 7 on crowd psychology.)

It is true that some types of investments are riskier than others, and that is why you should narrow your focus to maybe 5 per cent of all that is available in the securities markets, and forget the rest. When corporate bond funds pay more than funds invested in UK Government gilts, it is because you are assuming greater risk of making a wrong judgement for extra reward. For some of you it would be rational to take that extra risk to achieve your goals, for others it would be just silly. You have to weigh the risk of the investment in question against the risk of doing nothing, or failing to meet your goal and thus not fulfilling your obligations and responsibilities. Your gameplan should be clear and rational so that you feel confident and comfortable when implementing it.

CASE STUDY
Josh and Alice

Josh and Alice have two needs: to pay off their £150,000 mortgage, due in thirteen years, and to pay for private education for their two small children, Harriet aged nearly three and Henry who is six months. Clearly the mortgage isn't going to be a problem so their main objective is to create real wealth. They have the time, and enough disposable income and discipline to systematically save £10,000 jointly a year (after tax) to build a fund that could well be worth £600,000 plus in thirteen years' time.

Here is how. Josh, is a high flyer in his mid-thirties, employed in the compliance department of an investment bank in the City. His gameplan is to stay locked into the joint PEPs he and Alice own (four each), currently worth £109,000, and which are concentrated in the shares of growth companies based in the UK and in Europe, and also to invest the maximum allowed in Maxi-**ISAs** (a tax sheltered wrapper into which each can put a maximum of £7,000 in shares in 1999/2000 and £5,000 maximum thereafter) every tax year for the next thirteen.

The couple will sell enough of these holdings to pay off their interest-only mortgage when it is due. They will not have to pay tax on the proceeds because PEPs and Maxi-ISAs shelter them from **capital gains tax**. Josh reckons they will have more than enough left in their joint (tax sheltered) equity funds to put their children through private education and on to university one day.

Josh and Alice have calculated that in thirteen years, they will have invested £134,000 of capital into shares via Maxi-ISAs (£7,000 x 2 in 1999/2000 = £14,000, plus £10,000 jointly per tax year for the remaining twelve years within their time frame = £120,000). Also, in the past four years they have put £72,000 (£9,000, the maximum each allowed, x 4 = 8 PEPs, costing £72,000). Therefore over the seventeen years of funding they will have invested £134,000 + £72,000 = £206,000 in growth shares.

They know that there will be bad years, and sharp corrections, when the value of their shares may fall. Some of their shares will recover in due course, and others may not. Josh has watched enough ultra-bright fund managers at the office get a few things wrong in his time, so he knows no-one can get every stock pick right. But thanks to the bull market of 1995/8, Josh and Alice are off to a cracking start, with their fund currently worth £109,000 – two thirds of the value of their mortgage.

Josh is confident they will make a fortune, especially if the market falls temporarily and they could buy more shares at lower prices. He is right. While nothing is guaranteed in investment, and the value of shares can go down, as well as up, there is a good chance that if they stick to their gameplan, and reinvest all the dividends from their shares into more growth shares, they can meet their goal: to treble their total outlay in thirteen years' time. That is even after allowing for management costs, and bad years. That will leave them laughing when it comes to paying off their mortgage with tax-free proceeds from some of their PEPs and ISAs. They should not have to cash out more than a quarter or a third of their total holdings by then.

Harriet and Henry will have started secondary school, and Josh and Alice will have more than enough capital left in their fund, growing tax-free, to see their children through university. Josh and Alice will have achieved their goal to create wealth, and satisfied their needs without undue risk.

We can see that Josh and Alice can afford to adopt an aggressive investment strategy and go for above average growth because they have the time to ride out downturns, and are well placed to meet their future obligations. They have also finessed their gameplan by investing through tax sheltered vehicles – PEPs and ISAs. That makes sense because they are likely to remain in a higher rate tax bracket. This way they do not need to worry about capital gains tax going forward (at least not for the ten-year reprieve from tax on ISAs that the Government has promised), and if ever they could afford to invest even more in the market, say when Alice goes back to work as a computer software designer, they could buy shares outside the ISAs and use their joint CGT exemptions to deal tax-free.

If you are feeling despondent and thinking that is all very well for City yuppies like Josh, remember we are aiming to revolutionise your aspirations in this book. Stop thinking in terms of what you cannot do, and think big.

CASE STUDY
Billy and Suzy

Billy is in his early sixties and plans to retire from his job as company secretary of a local firm in three years. He has an inflation-proofed occupational pension that will pay two thirds of his final salary – some £32,000 before tax. Suzy has never worked. Their three children are independent and two are married. One has a child, aged four years. Billy and Suzy risk a fall in their standard of living in future unless they do something now to boost their investment income from their joint £75,000 in deposits, PEPs and various privatisation shares. They cannot afford to lose money in the short to medium term, and thus reduce the capital base from which they can earn more income to bump up Billy's pension. They have adequate life insurance and long term healthcare protection thanks to Bill's paternalistic firm.

Their need, and their goal, is to earn more income in three years' time, without risk of capital loss now. It would be irrational for them to do a Josh and Alice and rely entirely on growth shares via Maxi-ISAs over the next three years. They need a gameplan that protects a high proportion of their joint savings from capital loss and inflation, but also puts smaller amounts, say £4,000 each per year, making £24,000 over the next three years, into growth shares via Maxi-ISAs which they should hold for at least five years. The added attraction of Maxi-ISAs for this couple is that they are flexible, unlike a pension. They can cash out, tax-free, if they need the money. Billy and Suzy should not put money directly into individual shares, like Josh and Alice do, but they should spread their risks by investing in a fund of fifty or so blue chip businesses and in low cost index funds.

It would also be a good idea for Billy and Suzy to unlock the profit from their home, by selling their five bedroom, edge-of-town freehold house – the mortgage was paid off six years ago – and moving into a brand new flat in the centre. Suzy obtained an informal valuation for their house and was thrilled to learn it is worth £385,000 – maybe a little more. The flat would cost £160,000, would be much cheaper to run than their house, and it would also enhance their lifestyle. By moving they would have a net capital of around £220,000 tax-free (after 1 per cent stamp duty and other costs) which could go into a mix of Maxi-ISAs and collective funds invested for capital growth and more income.

Both these caricature couples are taking risks, but they are calculated risks designed to achieve their objectives. Risk is inherent in all wealth creation, but you are in control – you can choose low growth/low risk investments, or you can go for a high level of risk – but it should depend on your goals, not your emotional range.

It is a useful exercise to identify the kind of personality you are. See if you recognise yourself in any of the following categories.

Personality 1

- You are insecure, lack confidence and prone to irrational pessimism.
- You do not cross the road until the green light flashes, even when cars have stopped.
- You look left and right at railway lines, even when the barrier is up.
- You double check you have switched off the oven and unplugged the TV before you leave the house.
- You read articles on illnesses, and then imagine you have the symptoms.
- You always seek a second opinion, and even a third, on any commitment.

- You carry huge bunches of keys in your back pocket or briefcase.
- You do not really trust anyone – but are you right to trust yourself?
- You are prone to paranoia – and imagine everyone is out to rip you off.

If you can see yourself in more than half of the above statements then you probably have a RISK AVERSE personality. With regard to your finances you probably:

- Keep most of your money in short to medium term savings – bank and building society deposits; National Savings; income funds.
- Like to have complete control over, and instant access to, your money.

Personality 2

- You dislike surprises, and prefer to plan well in advance of any event such as a trip, party or meeting.
- You are not particularly curious – what you do not know is of no interest.
- You are meticulous about filing papers, mending/cleaning clothes/car.
- You think of yourself as a balanced, well-organised person, with self-control.
- You rarely eat or drink too much, and have never tried any illegal substances.
- You are a slave to routine: your watch, lists and diary rule your life.
- You suppress any intuitive responses and always try to remain rational.
- You are confident, but not very demanding, in your personal goals.

Find yourself agreeing with more than half of the above and the chances are you have a CONSERVATIVE personality. If this is the case then maybe you manage your money as follows:

- You have invested about half your funds in UK and European blue chip shares directly via PEPs and in collective funds through unit trusts. The rest is in capital safe savings.
- You are a cautious soul, not prone to impulse purchases or risky investments.

But beware! In being so careful you are carelessly letting opportunities pass you by.

Personality 3

- You ski off-piste, even when there is danger of avalanches.
- You buy securities 'on margin'.
- You are often late, and accelerate between speed cameras when driving.
- Your life is a series of deadlines – you thrive on pressure.
- You get a kick out of living life on the edge.
- You are extreme in your habits – feast and famine are more fun than moderation.
- You are fun to be with and on everyone's party list.
- You are long on enthusiasm/energy but display irrational exhuberance when investing.

If this sounds like you then you have an AGGRESSIVE personality. You probably have the following approach to your finances:

- You like small cap. stocks, Internet and biotechnology shares.
- You have written off substantial capital losses against future profits.
- You see little point in buying blue chips when you can double or treble up in start-up companies, and specialist funds invested in bombed out emerging markets and other recovery situations.
- You are somewhat naïve and crave break-neck excitement and could also be a little cocky about your machismo.

But remember, testosterone does not make up for losses and unless you are also a masochist, losses are no fun.

Get your *real* priorities right

These are of course cartoon sketches used to illustrate the extremes of different personalities. As we have discussed above, you must first identify your goals, that is the priorities in your long term investment plan. Then you can equate that goal with the risk you will have to sustain in order to attain it. Sometimes, as in the case of Josh and Alice, an aggressive strategy is a sensible choice. Now rate the following objectives in order of priority in your own financial gameplan. Put them into categories classified as:

Your priorities/long term goals – circle the appropriate rating

1. for **priority**
2. for **very important**
3. for **important**
4. for **not important**

	1	2	3	4
To protect your family should you die young	1	2	3	4
To build wealth now to retire before you are fifty	1	2	3	4
To build savings to invest lump sums in ISAs or house deposit	1	2	3	4
To protect earnings in case of sickness/disability/ illness	1	2	3	4
To extend/refurbish a property	1	2	3	4
To invest for maximum capital growth, but no income now	1	2	3	4
To invest for maximum income now/capital safety	1	2	3	4
To invest now for maximum future income	1	2	3	4
To invest now for any school fees payable in the future	1	2	3	4
To pool existing debts in one low cost card and pay it off	1	2	3	4
To remortgage for a better deal, even paying penalties	1	2	3	4
Protection against inheritance tax.	1	2	3	4
Growing capital and income for your retirement	1	2	3	4
To save up for a specific project	1	2	3	4
Others – specify	1	2	3	4

Once you have done this, try writing your own list – the precise goals which you perceive as your financial needs, and then rate these objectives in order of priority. This is a difficult exercise. You will not be able to reconcile all your *perceived needs* as '**1**'. Some objectives are going to have to go into '**2**'. When you have thought this through and are committed to the essential goals that are in your '**1**' category you are ready to quantify them and write your gameplan.

But first, another word about time. As we have discussed, time can reduce or increase your risk depending on how much time you have to achieve your particular goal.

If you have short term goals, you run higher risk of capital loss by investing in stocks and shares as market volatility can catch you on the back foot and you will be forced to sell when prices are low. So synchronise short term goals with short term investments that are capital safe. If you have long term objectives, like Josh and Alice, you can use time to compound your gains and to reduce your risk when investing in shares. Some years may be bad, but if you have the time to recover from the downturns you are still in control.

Again, you can only assess the risk in time by relating it to your goal. The longer you leave your money invested, the less control you have over it in theory, and the more you should expect to be rewarded for assuming that risk. But interest rates can fall, and/or inflation rise, and thus cheat you out of a satisfactory return over time. That is why short dated gilts are less risky than long. That is also why you normally should expect more interest on a six-month deposit than one with instant access.

Finally there is market timing: it does not work. In Step 5, I shall tell you how to take the guesswork out of trying to time the market with cost averaging – that is staggering your purchases of shares at regular intervals and in equal amounts.

Money begets money

No doubt by now you are thinking that it is all very well for well paid professionals and entrepreneurs in the cusp of their earning power: they can afford to invest regularly for future capital growth. They do not need income now and so are well placed to substantially increase their wealth. You are right – money begets money. But regular investment over a long period of time will compound the growth of the capital invested. The power of time to enhance investment performance and reduce risk cannot be overstated.

Patient and persistent investors with the luxury of time and income surplus to their requirements can make a substantial impact on their future wealth. Perhaps 10 per cent of your net earnings seems a lot to some of you, or perhaps it doesn't seem much to others, but as long as you keep pumping it into your fund every month, and ideally, reinvest the dividends, you will, over several years, create substantial real wealth out of net income.

When you begin to write your plan you should first look at your time scale. Whether long term – say five to ten years – or somewhat shorter, it is vital that you take inflation into account. While the risk of nominal loss of capital is reduced when asset backed investments are held over the long term, the real value – that is after taking inflation into account – is eroded by the annual rate of inflation. Over time, that inflation can seriously damage your wealth. Its corrosive power is very great in long term holdings of cash, which grow barely above inflation and tax. So you must ensure that all your investments earn a real return to create real wealth.

At the time of writing this book, we in the UK, Europe and US are basking in low inflation while our economies are still growing. But even relatively low inflation – when compared with the double-digit variety experienced in the UK in the 70s for example – can cut the purchasing power of your money at a frightening pace. At 2 per cent annual inflation, the purchasing power of your money is cut in half in thirty-four years. At 5 per cent it will take only fourteen years to halve and at 7 per cent just ten years.

AMOUNT	INFLATION	5 YEARS	10 YEARS	15 YEARS
10,000	2.5%	8,811	7,763	6,840
10,000	3.5%	8,368	7,003	5,860
10,000	5.0%	7,738	5,987	4,633

HOW INFLATION EATS INTO CAPITAL

That is awesome, and especially frightening for the retired who can now expect to live well into their eighties. Inflation is the enemy that we should all fear. Inflation puts risk into so-called capital safe investment, and in order to safeguard yourself against it, your long term gameplan must assume much higher inflation going forward (to be on the safe side) and embrace a substantial element of capital growth to mitigate against its corrosive power or else you will risk failing to achieve your goals because your purchasing power will have declined.

Another consideration when writing your plan is tax. Tax should not drive your investment choices but as you complete your plan, make sure that each calculation is based on money after tax. The tax-free wrapper of the Maxi-ISA is worth having. The Mini-ISAs, which allow small sums of cash and life insurance to be invested tax-free, are not very appealing as the costs are high and the returns low. The cocktail in a Mini-ISA will also erode the limit that you can invest in stocks and shares quoted on any exchange in the world via a Maxi-ISA. Even if you are a basic rate taxpayer now, given the long term time scale of your gameplan, go for this tax shelter and save a packet if you become a higher rate taxpayer later.

The tax shelter also allows you to use your annual capital gains tax allowance. If you can afford to invest both inside and outside the ISA, you can harvest up to £7,100 of free capital gains (in 1999/2000) outside the Maxi-ISA, while also benefitting from tax-free growth and capital gains within its tax-free zone. That is quite an incentive but you should remember that you can only carry capital losses forward against gains made *outside* the ISA. Capital gains from UK government gilts are tax-free – but losses cannot be discounted against your profits from other investments. Income tax is deducted at source on dividends and bank interest, along with the income from gilts.

In Step 4 the tax privileges accorded to investors in property are explained in detail. For those with little capital and lots of time, investment in property is ideal, for property can leverage capital substantially. For higher rate taxpayers with a large share portfolio and surplus income over their needs, investment property is an attractive diversification. But property has to be actively managed, whereas investment in stocks and shares can be relatively passive once you have done the groundwork in planning and the homework in research.

Now write your plan.

First identify your financial priorities, then:

1. Quantify the cost of implementing your plan.
2. Work out how to reallocate the sum from current expenditure/income.
3. Get the time scale right.
4. Eliminate investments least likely to achieve your goals – see Step 3.
5. Establish which investments might work, why, and how they could be funded.
6. Check out your assumptions with providers and/or an adviser.
7. Establish what the risks are.
8. If the risks are worth taking to reach your goal, then go ahead.
9. If the risks are unnecessary, go back to number 5 and write another plan.

Step 3

Your

Choices

Understand the broad options before
you take decisive action

STEP 3
Your Choices

Now that you have conditioned yourself to manage your finances more intelligently and written an investment plan to suit your needs we can take a look at the choices available to you.

However you decide to invest your money, you must take the time to understand the basic differences and characteristics of each generic product and service in order to ask providers appropriate questions and understand their answers. Once you have that basic knowledge, you will be able to shop wisely for what you need. The Financial Services Authority noted that:

> 'While those who provide financial products and services may understand the complexities of investment trusts versus unit trusts, **endowment** versus **repayment mortgages**, or **AVCs** versus **FSAVCs**, this is unfamiliar and unintelligible territory for many consumers. The financial services sector has had a tradition of producing confusing product literature, often written in unfamiliar language...'[1]

It is easy to be intimidated by the seeming complexity of financial services and the mystique surrounding them, but do not let providers or advisers fool you into thinking they are doing you a favour – it's the other way round. The people who want to borrow your money or to sell you their managed products, services or shares, have specific financial needs too. You as a client, or as a shareholder or bondholder, are satisfying *their* needs.

[1] November 1998 consultation paper

When, for example, a bank manager grants you a personal or business loan, it may seem as if he is the giver and you the taker in the relationship. Wrong. The cost of that loan – what you pay him – is the profit you give him and he needs that profit to grow his business. If you can understand the interests of the people who want to use your money, you will also be able to work out what is in it for you – you will learn to ignore what you do not need. But you cannot afford ignorance as you could then be sold the wrong products, or mix of products, and you would pay the real cost later.

Imagine yourself at a supermarket with tens of thousands of items on the shelves. Now see yourself at the checkout with a basket containing no more than twenty different products. What did you do? You zoomed in on what you needed, snatched up your chosen brand, and did not waste time looking at other types of products on offer. That is precisely what you will do when choosing among the various investment options in the market.

Use your money in three basic ways

You will know that to be physically fit you must eat a balance of foods that provide the six basic nutrients (protein, carbohydrate, fat, vitamins, minerals and water) which are essential for energy and good health. Well in the same way, to be financially fit you should use your money to:

- Secure protection of capital.
- Generate income from capital.
- Invest for capital growth.

Or, a fourth option is to mix the last two, with emphasis on one or other or a balance of both.

When you buy financial products and services you have consumer rights and economic power – learn to use them. Ensure you know what you want, you are clear about what you are getting, and the offer is good value, that is, of quality but also competitive in price. Learn to probe, to compare, to negotiate and, if necessary, to complain. The financial services industry is highly regulated to protect private investors. But knowledge is protection and financial education is woefully lacking.

Before you invest, investigate

Ask questions, no matter how basic, before you buy. Take notes and let the providers know you are. Should you go ahead with them, insist that first they confirm in writing the cost, access, tax, risk, restrictions/penalties of the investment or service.

No-one can legislate to protect you against your own ignorance or bad judgement, but if you have reason to complain about misinformation, overcharging or mis-selling, write to the compliance officer of the company involved. He must respond and compensate you or else face hefty fines and damage to his reputation. If you do not get a response, write to the regulator that authorises the said provider. The regulator's name will be on the provider's letterhead. Meticulously record financial correspondence/transactions in case of complaints and for tax purposes.

You cannot afford inertia

Whether you are juggling debt or high disposable income, do not be daunted by the apparent complexity of financial products and services and, rather than risk taking the wrong decision, do nothing. Inertia is a dangerous state of mind in money management. The risk is you will lose financial fitness and may become vulnerable.

Misguided loyalty is another emotion you cannot afford when it comes to managing your money. Just because you have always been with a certain building society or bank, or your mortgage lender is a nice chap, it does not necessarily follow that they will be in a position to offer you the best deal and service, or even that you can trust them. Keep monitoring what is available in the market, and if your provider does not match the best deals going, withdraw your economic power and plug it in elsewhere.

Lack of basic knowledge of money management leads us all to put off making financial decisions until we are forced to focus on our circumstances. Life-changing events tend to force financial decisions upon us. Meanwhile we procrastinate, unable to assess the risks/rewards of financial transactions we may undertake.

Notably, inheritance can either kick-start you in creation of future wealth or it can be a squandered opportunity. Money begets money, so do not waste the opportunity handed down to you to invest a lump sum in a pension, property or shares. Make full use of the money to build wealth, which you can eventually pass down to the next generation.

Personal investment planning ought to be a compulsory GCSE subject – it is as essential as the three Rs. It may pay the advice industry to mystify investment: it will certainly pay you to learn how to get your head around it. Once you understand the basic investment concepts, you will be able to categorise even complex investment products, just as you would skip the meat counter in a supermarket if you are vegetarian.

Successful investment is based on choosing the right pick and mix of options within the two positions identified in Step 1 in order to achieve your goals without taking unnecessary risk. In case you need reminding, you can either be a lender, or an owner.

So far, perhaps, you have worked for your money but your money has not worked for you. But now you are changing your thinking and beginning to condition yourself, you can take action to put your money out to work. You will give it specific tasks and make sure it completes those jobs efficiently and cost-effectively.

How to use your money

USE	COMMENT	POTENTIAL RETURN	POTENTIAL RISK
Spend it	Good fun but suspends wealth creation.	None	None
Hoard and hide it	Irrational, and risks loss through theft and/or inflation.	None	High

USE	COMMENT	POTENTIAL RETURN	POTENTIAL RISK
Lend it to a bank, building society or post office	Earn meagre returns.	Low	Low
Lend it to governments (bonds/gilts)	Risk capital loss unless held to redemption.	Low/Med	Low/Med
Lend it to companies (corporate bonds)	Various capital risk ratings, but 'secure' income. Some inflation risk.	Medium	Medium
Own funds in fixed income securities	Risk to capital.	Medium	Medium
Own funds in shares	Short term risk of price volatility/ loss and possibly bad fund management performance.	Medium	Medium
Life insurance: with-profits investment	If regular premium = low growth, high cost, low return.	Low/Med	Low/Med
Life insurance: unit-linked investment	Provides market-linked performance – at high cost.	Medium	Medium
Own pension policies	Maxi tax relief, mini flexibility/ no control over 75 per cent of capital.	Medium	Medium
Own shares	Various risks but potential high reward.	High	High
Own property	Residence and/or investment. Costly to hold and can be hard to sell quickly.	Medium	Medium
Own a business	Long hours, hassle, and risk but can be ultimately rewarding, financially and personally.	Low – High	Low – High
Own horses, art, antiques, vintage cars, jewellery	For enthusiasts/specialists only.	High	High
Gamble	Stake money on lady luck – and risk losing all.	Low – High	High

Note: If the risk is higher than the return, the investment is unlikely to meet your needs.

These are of course broad options and there is a vast array of variations on them. These variations include oeics (pronounced 'oiks' and standing for **open-ended investment companies**), futures, options, **warrants**, preferred shares, **derivatives**, and along with ordinary shares there are convertible loan stock, junk bonds, **annuities**, **hedge funds** and so on. These instruments are designed to suit specific needs. As with everything, there is quality and there is junk within each of these investment options. Derivatives and hedge funds, for example, have had a bad press (remember Nick Leeson who was jailed in Singapore when his doomed derivative trading brought down Barings in 1994). They are reputed to be high risk, but are not necessarily – it depends on how they are used and by whom, to meet which specific needs.

Hedge fund managers are contrarian creatures who essentially bet on what they perceive to be temporary (mis) pricing in the securities markets. A quality hedge fund can prove an excellent investment – although even the brightest fund managers can also lose all your money. In late 1998, Long Term Capital Management (LTCM) headed by former Salomon Bros. whizz kid John Meriwhether, was all but wiped out and had to be rescued. For all the elegant maths of the fund managers – among them two Nobel Prize winners, and not a few PhDs in mathematics and finance – their computer driven trading strategy was not bullet-proof. They had over-leveraged and lacked the single most crucial necessity for any investor, whether private or professional: staying power. After a cash bail out, LTCM was able to rebuild its fortunes.

Leave out exotic ingredients from a plain vanilla wealth plan

Most amateur private investors should stick to a plain vanilla wealth creation plan and leave out such exotic ingredients as derivatives and hedge funds. But if you are comfortable investing in sophisticated securities and instruments or have an adviser able to evaluate your risk/reward in relation to your objectives, then go ahead. Your plan should be your own, written by you or for you, and only you or your adviser can ultimately decide how to implement it. But why take extra risk to attain your goal if you do not need to? As we established in Step 2, the mere assumption of greater investment risk does not guarantee greater rewards. It is not that simple.

Your investment risks should be a rational calculation, based on your financial needs. Apply the broad investment concepts that are best suited to meet those needs. You don't need to prove anything, your task is to meet your objectives, so avoid gratuitous risk. Nothing is certain in investment, but the discipline of risk reduction will avoid mistakes and so limit the damage and give you confidence to persist with your plan.

Choose your product carefully

How much you put into shares as opposed to bonds, cash or property is a calculation each individual must make according to his or her 'sleep well ratio' or investment personality, immediate to medium term needs for income and capital growth and long term financial goals. Even someone earning monthly income way above their monthly expenditure may not have the temperament to adopt an aggressive wealth creation strategy and prefer instead to invest through conservatively managed funds run by insurance companies or unit trusts.

The managed funds run by insurance companies are supposedly ultra-conservative in their mix of fixed income securities, cash, shares and property. But the asset mix of a with-profits fund is similar to that of any managed fund with some 60 per cent invested in shares and the remainder in bonds, property and cash. Life insurance companies are increasingly competing head to head with unit and investment trust fund managers for market share in the wealth creation industry. They are under pressure to improve their performance and cut their charges for fund management.

In the retirement savings market for example, insurance companies offer innovative products such as **variable annuities**, which are not only skewed to interest rates but also to the performance of the stock market. The major life insurance companies exude awesome financial strength and are well placed to (hard) sell long term investment products in life insurance wrappers. But they do not necessarily offer the best investment choices – particularly in slow-earn, low-return regular premium products; or if policies are not run to maturity and heavy penalties are charged.

Buy the most potent product to satisfy each need

The insurance industry in the United Kingdom drives a large section of the financial planning industry, even though insurance products are not pure investments. Once upon a time, premiums for life insurance in the UK were tax-deductible and the habit of 'investing' in life assurance has stuck. But insurance products with investment components such as **with-profits** endowments, **whole of life** policies and **single premium bonds** may not provide the best return. Not that an intelligently run insurance company cannot produce good investment returns, but that their costs are prohibitively high and often absorb a big chunk of dividends and capital gains.

So the best investment policy is not to mix your life insurance and investment needs in one product. Such hybrids are often complex and inflexible with heavy management charges and sales commissions. Put your money into a well managed investment fund and buy cheap term insurance if you also need life cover.

It may be comforting to pay regular premiums to a life company, and thus to invest automatically. The discipline of persistent investment is good. But what is bad is that some insurance products are encumbered by heavy sales commissions and possible penalties and may not live up to your investment expectations. Products such as **endowments** demand a long gestation and are often used, along with an interest-only loan to support house purchase. Yet such plans do not guarantee return of your mortgage borrowings – unless you die! Insurance funds are most unlikely to beat the growth of a well managed equity fund held over the same number of years. There may be less capital risk in insurance funds but there is greater risk of underperformance. Moreover, their taxation treatment may not be making the best use of your capital gains tax allowances.

Investment products offered by insurance companies

- Endowments.
- Single premium bonds.
- Whole of life insurance.
- Annuities.
- Guaranteed income bonds.
- Personal pension plans.

Not all of the above are the most suitable for real wealth creation. However, annuities and personal pension plans are major components of personal pension investment. For detailed discussion of the advantages and disadvantages, see Pensions section on p.63.

Go for maximum flexibility in an unstable world

The Government has promised to introduce a more flexible 'stakeholder pension' in 2001 and in the meantime has warned people to watch out for penalties they may suffer if they switch from ordinary regular premium pension plans to a stakeholder plan. That is because regular premium pension plans were invariably 'front end loaded' – that is your premiums in the early years paid for charges and sales commissions. That effectively deprived your fund of the potency of early premiums, which if invested in their entirety, produced a greater performance than the premiums paid into it in later years.

If you bought a regular premium product and switched within a couple of years to say a stakeholder scheme, your fund would almost certainly be worth less than the sum of your contributions because the provider and salesman would have paid themselves upfront. The planned introduction of stakeholder pensions and the effective government wealth warning has had a beneficial effect on these charges.

But all the same, check the 'key features' document carefully to see the effect of charges on future performance if you are thinking of investing in a personal pension.

To sum up, insurance products (notably with-profits endowments and whole of life insurance) with an investment component may not be suitable for wealth creation because:

- Charges: high sales commissions traditionally paid to sales people are ultimately paid by you.
- Insurance funds are conservatively managed: too conservatively for high performance wealth creation.
- Packaging: you may be paying for features you don't need.
- Lack of flexibility: regular premium with-profits contracts are very poor value for money unless you maintain them to maturity – typically ten years or more.
- With-profits policies are opaque: only highly trained actuaries understand how bonuses – paid annually and at maturity – are calculated.

You cannot look up the value of your regular premium endowments, pension policies and whole of life products each day while you hold them. But if you could, you might be appalled to see how poor the returns are from regular premium policies – particularly in the early years. Indeed, never surrender an endowment before maturity: if in dire need of cash you could raise a loan from the provider or auction it in the market. An alternative would be to take a bank loan against your policy and continue with it. All your options need to be finally assessed if you find yourself in this situation.

Risk aversion – the paler shade of fear – is often brought into the sales pitch by insurance salesmen: they argue that their products are 'safe', 'tax-efficient' (that usually means tax-paid, not tax-free), and conservatively managed. Private investors can thus be lulled into a false sense of security and think they are investing in a 'safe' method by which to repay the mortgage, or whatever other financial goal they have to meet far into the future. But a coherent investment plan based on investment in blue chip shares held for the long term will perform better in terms of capital growth, and transaction costs can be kept to a minimum, so your returns are not eroded as they are with an insurance/investment product.

So buy the most potent products to satisfy your needs separately and beware the empty allure of cross-selling as banks, building societies, life companies, brokers/asset managers, even the blessed Marks & Spencer and Virgin try to persuade us that one-stop shopping for financial services is best. Best for whom? Remember we are the givers, and the providers of financial services are the takers. Always keep an eye on who benefits from what.

Hierarchy of financial needs

The Chartered Insurance Institute, in its coursebook for budding independent financial advisers, argues that the hierarchy of financial needs is as follows:

- Financial protection against death.
- Financial protection against disability and critical illness.
- Mortgage repayments.
- Pension provision.
- Savings for non-pension purposes.
- Investment.

My own investment strategy recognises those needs but puts them in reverse priority. Only those with dependants and large financial liabilities must have life insurance as a number '**1**' in the scale of priorities. In my investment philosophy, systematic investment of part of your earnings each month is 'paying yourself first'. That is not to say that you might not need also to pay your life insurance premiums, mortgage and pension contributions each month but that investment in your future wealth and from that, the ability to satisfy your financial needs, is a '**1**'. Investment is not the least essential need, but an absolute necessity.

   A sensible investment plan, systematically implemented, should, after several years, create a capital fund to repay your financial liabilities and meet commitments such as the mortgage, children's education and the cost of care in your old age. How much you put into your investment fund and at what stage in your life you start to work up your financial fitness will determine your future wealth. Let us discuss the three basic objectives of savings and investments in greater detail.

1. Capital protection

The most common investments that safeguard your capital are:

- Bank and building society savings accounts.
- Money market funds.
- Unit trusts invested in cash and short term loans to government.
- Post Office savings accounts.
- Tax-free National Savings certificates – five-year term.

The risks in the above lie in the long term, because of rising inflation and/or variable interest rates, but they are valid in the following circumstances:

- Instantly accessible emergency fund.
- Deposit on a property that you are about to buy.
- Funds to pay large bills, due shortly, such as school fees or purchase of car.
- Savings of elderly people who want fixed monthly income without risk.

When you invest for protection, your '**1**' priority is safety and your objective is to conserve what you have. Your choices are largely limited to lending your money for relatively short periods for instant, one month, 60 or 90 days access and then only to reputable borrowers such as the major banks, building societies and the Post Office. Your capital will be safe only in nominal terms, and you will sacrifice the higher returns you could have made if you had lent it for longer periods or placed it in riskier forms of lending. Moreover, unless you earn enough to cover the annual rate of inflation you will not even protect the purchasing power of your money. As stressed in Step 2, you must think in terms of real return – that is the return after inflation is deducted – not just nominal return when evaluating how much you can earn on your money.

When interest rates are low, the nominal return will seem depressingly low. But you must work out what you are getting in real terms, compared with what you might get in, say, government or corporate bonds. Bonds might look more attractive than cash or shares when they offer a yield higher than the rate of inflation, but bonds also carry greater risk of capital loss than cash unless you hold them to redemption.

Money is a commodity, and those who would borrow yours are professional lenders. The lenders use your money to fashion 'value added' loans to business users. They might charge small and/or leveraged companies up to 4 per cent more for loans than they pay you to borrow your savings. Efficient companies consistently earn high double-digit returns on the capital they employ in their businesses and are deemed financially secure, so borrow for less. But still the banks earn profits by recycling your deposits into corporate loans.

As a private investor, you will only grow real wealth by investing your capital in shares of highly efficient businesses; not by depositing it into savings accounts at barely enough return to cover inflation and tax. Nor can you be sure of earning a constant rate of interest on instantly accessible bank deposits. The banks offer variable rates of interest, that is they move their rates up and down according to base rates. You can secure fixed rates, but only by lending your money out for longer, losing flexibility and taking greater risk on inflation.

Example – The risk of inflation

If you deposited £10,000 at 4 per cent gross interest a year, and inflation (the rise in the retail price index) was 2.5 per cent a year, you would earn a 'real return' of only 1.5 per cent before tax. And as if that were not bad enough, here is the real rub: tax is deducted from gross income, not from the real return. So if you were a basic rate taxpayer, 20 per cent income tax would be deducted from the £400 gross interest paid on your £10,000 deposit (at 4 per cent). That would leave you with £320, net of tax, after a year – a real return of just £70.

Why £70? Well, because your £10,000 would have been eroded in purchasing power by inflation at 2.5 per cent. By the end of the year it can buy only £9,750 worth of goods and services. Inflation of 2.5 per cent has put prices up and shrunk your capital by corresponding amounts. Net income on your deposit of £320 makes up for the shrinkage, but reduces your real profit to £70, or 0.7 per cent of the £10,000 deposited at 4 per cent per year.

If you are a higher rate tax payer, you would derive only £240 in net income, after paying 40 per cent tax. With the £250 shrinkage in your £10,000, your *loss* in real terms would be £10, or 0.1 per cent, after one year. Hardly surprisingly, many wealthy savers keep some cash in five-year inflation-proofed, tax-free National Savings certificates, or even premium bonds: they can offer better returns to higher rate tax payers.

The advantage of investment for capital protection is liquidity – that is the ability to access your cash quickly. Bank and building society deposit accounts can be instantly accessible, or if held on longer terms of notice, higher interest is paid, although penalties are levied if you withdraw the funds before maturity. When you sell shares, bonds or collective investments, it normally takes five working days to get the cash (but you must also **settle** within that time if you buy them). Property is of course very illiquid due to the length of time it normally takes to sell it, and receive the proceeds.

2. Earn income

Investments that allow you to earn income include:

- Government and local authority bonds including index-linked gilts.
- Utility stocks – shares in water, electricity or gas companies yield high dividends.
- Annuities.
- National Savings accounts and bonds.
- Guaranteed income bonds.
- Corporate bonds, whether high-grade (Triple A) or 'junk' variety.
- Unit/investment trusts invested in fixed income securities.
- Shares that pay high dividends.
- Letting a room in your home – under the rent-a-room scheme this is tax-free to a limit of £4,250 gross p.a. (1999–2000).
- Fully let commercial property with ten years or more unexpired on lease.

Your '**1**' priority is to earn maximum income from your capital without undue risk, although you need to be prepared to assume more risk than when investing for protection. You are still essentially a lender (unless you buy commercial property or high yielding shares), but you are lending your money out in return for the guarantee of a relatively secure, predictable income stream that may outpace prevailing inflation, and which is more than you would get from pure protection investments. The longer you lend out your money, the more you should expect to earn on it.

For example, long-dated gilts (UK government bonds) normally pay higher rates of interest than shorts because you would hold them for longer to redemption, when you would receive nominal or face value. In the meantime you sustain the risk of capital loss as the price fluctuates on the market, driven by supply/demand. You get an extra reward for assuming higher risk for longer.

There is a degree both of capital risk and income risk in all of the above listed income-driven investments (except perhaps the rent-a-room scheme, see details below). With gilts, the risk is low if held to redemption but corporate bonds are far riskier and most are less liquid than gilts. Companies that offer suspiciously high dividends are often ex-growth, and not safe to buy-and-hold over the long term. That category does not include great growth companies that pay low percentage yields in dividends, but regularly increase the amount of payout.

Well let commercial property in the late 90s offered outstanding value with net yields of 8 per cent a year. But rental income from property eventually converts into capital growth, so commercial property is not purely geared to future income. Property has a greater affinity with growth shares than with bonds but it can be a high-income investment and a valid option for investors who need to supplement, or to replace, earned income with regular investment income. Rent from commercial property is paid in advance once a quarter (see Step 4).

Investments for income have the following attractions:

- Capital gains on gilts are free of tax.
- Liquidity is good in gilts, collective investments and company shares.
- Low cost dealing in government gilts.
- Capital and income is inflation-proofed in index-linked gilts.
- Corporate/convertible bonds are higher yield but riskier and less liquid than gilts.
- Good investments in deflationary times.
- Can provide regular income stream for the retired or to supplement salary.

3. Grow capital

In order to grow capital your best options are shares, property and/or your own business. **Asset backed investments** will appreciate or decrease in value to reflect their perceived earnings prospects. The higher risk inherent in ownership of asset backed investments should be rewarded by higher returns provided you make the right choices of what to buy and hold over say ten years or longer. Shares have consistently produced the highest real returns compared with bonds and cash, if held for several years. They can perform badly for periods of time and in the short term their prices are highly volatile. They can also fall in sudden and shocking market declines but for private investors who want to create wealth long term the greatest risk is to be out of the stock market.

AMOUNT	RETURN	5 YEARS	10 YEARS	15 YEARS
10,000	5.0%	12,763	16,289	20,789
10,000	8.0%	14,693	21,589	31,722
10,000	10.0%	16,105	25,937	41,772
10,000	12.0%	17,623	31,058	54,736

HOW COMPOUND GROWTH CAN CREATE REAL WEALTH

Collective investments

Collective investments such as unit and investment trusts and open-ended investment companies (oeics), which are a hybrid of the two, offer you diversification in your investment portfolio without having to select shares in different companies for yourself. Professional investment managers decide what shares or bonds to buy and sell and when to do it. You pay a management fee for that service on what is known as a discretionary basis, which means you have no say in what they do with your money.

The personal finance industry promotes diversified investment in 50 shares or more held in collective investments. They are called collective because investors' money is pooled in a large portfolio of investments

managed by professionals who have discretion to make all the investment decisions. Each investor has a direct stake in the vehicle that
holds and manages these investments. Units in unit trusts reflect the
precise underlying valuation of the shares in the pooled fund.

By contrast, investment trusts are companies whose share prices go
up and down according to investor demand, and can either trade at a
discount or a premium of the value of the shares in which they invest.

In the 1974 **bear market** discounts were as wide as 45 per cent,
although they have narrowed to well under 10 per cent in recent years.
Premiums add additional uncertainty to investment trust shares, while
discounts add spice. Investment trusts are increasingly sold as better
value in terms of costs than unit trusts.

The relatively high cost of professional management fees and the
bid/offer spreads you pay when you buy and sell unit trusts are the subject of not a little whinging. However that cost can be minimal if you
buy through a discount broker, while the cost of frequent trading of
directly held shares through a stockbroker can be about the same as
buying unit trusts. For most investors the simplest way to participate in
the growth of great businesses quoted on the stock market is to buy
units or shares in collective investments. Funds invested in world class
businesses that adhere to the tenets in Step 5 are the right choice for a
long term growth strategy.

Super-charged fees for pedestrian performance

A piece of research, undertaken for the **Financial Services Authority**
(FSA) estimated that high investment management charges seriously
eroded the returns from capital invested in professionally-managed
funds. There are two main categories of costs:

1. The transaction fees and front-end or back-end loads paid when you buy,
   sell or switch funds.
2. The ongoing management fees.

The FSA did not publish the highly critical paper because howls of
protests from unit trust and life assurance lobbies threw doubt on its
accuracy. But it touched a raw nerve. The fund management industry is
acutely aware that if future returns from stocks and shares fall below

the extraordinary heights reached in recent years, its charges will be exposed to greater scrutiny and measured against performance. Increased competition and consumer awareness will force down charges at collective funds, while exceptional fund managers well deserve superior rewards.

Costs matter because they erode your investment returns. A collective fund with high expenses and a **front-end load** will have to perform that much better than a low-cost fund. No-one would begrudge turbo-charged fees for super-charged performance but you should baulk at paying high management charges on your pension or unit trust contributions in exchange for poor or pedestrian performance. Choose your investment manager wisely as a good one will make you more money than you could ever make on your own.

Track the prices and performance of leading unit and investment trusts recorded over 1, 3 and 10 years in the *Financial Times*. Their **volatility** is also rated, giving you an indication of their risk rating. Now that you read *FT Money* every Saturday without fail, you know where to find the tables showing winners and losers. When you are familiar with the different types you will be ready to start shopping for a collective fund that best suits your needs.

Collective funds are designated according to their respective investment objectives, such as:

- UK Growth.
- UK Growth & Income.
- UK Smaller Companies.
- UK Equity Income.
- Far East ex Japan.
- Global Emerging Markets.
- Property.
- Commodity & Energy.

The risk in the underlying funds is generally perceived (in descending order) as:

- Specialist funds (i.e. global emerging markets).
- General equity funds (UK growth and income).
- Fund of funds (a pick and mix of different funds as opposed to shares).
- Property funds.

- Managed funds (a mix of 60 per cent shares, the rest in gilts, cash and property).
- Building society funds.
- Cash or deposit funds.

The key questions to ask before you buy are:
- How has this fund performed, compared to its peers, in the past five years?
- Who is the fund manager and how long has he or she been there?
- Does the fund match my investment goal – would my money be doing the right job?
- How will this fund make money for me – income, capital growth, interest?
- How much will I be charged when I buy, and what are the ongoing expenses?
- What are the specific risks in this fund? (Ask the provider, and a competitor.)
- What securities does the fund hold, and how often does it change strategy?
- Is the fund 'laced' with higher risk securities such as derivatives/junk bonds?

If possible, it is also valuable to get an unbiased evaluation of performance/risk of the fund.

Volatility

The economic/business environment is constantly changing and with it the volatility of different types of funds. That is why it makes sense for long term investors to buy unit trusts or investment trusts invested in global businesses to spread the risk geographically.

Volatility is not of itself risky but is dangerous when it destabilises investor psychology and causes panic, whether in buying or selling. There was a downward spiral in confidence amid acute volatility and sharp falls on world stock markets in September/October 1998. Alan Greenspan, chairman of the US Federal Reserve Board cut interest rates to shore up liquidity and confidence. Other central banks followed. The strategy worked. It was not done by magic; the fundamentals of the US economy were sound, and as earnings in the first quarter of 1999 came in higher than early gloomy expectations, money poured back into stocks and shares.

The media dramatise the inherent volatility of stock markets with shock words and graphics that promote fear of buying shares. On the contrary, extraordinary shares will generate growth in income and capital and greatly enhance your future finances. Historically, one could conservatively expect average growth of 8 to 10 per cent a year from blue chip shares, and in good economic times, much better. Outstanding growth businesses should maintain at least this average pace of growth even when less robust businesses cannot.

It is also worth remembering that professional fund managers are not bound by any means to be better than you at investment. Indeed they often do worse than private investors who stick to a good capital growth strategy such as that highlighted in Step 5. So if you have sufficient capital and confidence to build your own portfolio of 8 to 12 directly held shares, go ahead. But as explained later, narrow your focus to shares in world class growth businesses.

In Step 5 the merits of regular investment to average out your cost whether in direct investment in shares or via unit trusts and investment trusts, is also explained. This way you stagger your purchases into the market to average out your cost. You also put into place a persistent savings plan by investing the same amount in the same securities at regular intervals. You would automatically buy more when the market is down, and less when it is up. It takes the guesswork out of when to buy.

Diversification does not guarantee lower risk/higher performance

Clearly collective investments are safer because the risk of losing capital in shares is spread over a diversified portfolio. It is putting your eggs into several baskets. The conventional view is that direct investment in a few exceptional shares – as advocated in Step 5 – is too risky for all but the very wealthy who can 'afford to lose'. But direct investment may not be riskier than collective investments while it certainly can be more profitable.

Listen to the spiel of a leading investment manager:

'Very few people have the time or resources to research individual stocks [shares] and everyone knows it is dangerous to put all your eggs in one basket. [Our] funds generally invest in the shares of at least 50 companies and sometimes as many as 200, where added diversity not only makes good investment sense but also reduces risk.'

Diversification may indeed reduce investment risk, but it also reduces reward, and as such it is a doubled-edged sword. Collective investments are usually too diversified to achieve outstanding performance. Indeed, only a small proportion of them beat the leading stock market indices. So although collective investments may be the most practical choice for most of you who want to own shares, be careful to choose a fund for its strategy, and potential superior performance – and not just because it is diversified.

Quality not quantity is what counts

If you directly held sixteen shares, you would not have 100 per cent more security than if you held eight shares. Indeed too much diversification, as advocated by those selling funds invested in 50 to 200 shares, dilutes potential profits. Such sales pitches for collective investments pander to private investors' insecurities about direct investment in shares and serve to mystify the so-called 'art' of investment management. But if you take the time to learn how to identify superior companies, and avoid all the rest, you are likely to derive better than average returns from directly owning shares, without undue risk (see Step 5).

Pensions

Your future financial strength depends on your ability to grow capital, whether through a pension or through investment in shares and/or property. (See Step 4 and Step 5.) Pensions benefit from tax relief on contributions, but company pensions excepted, they can be inflexible, costly and, given low annuity rates, ultimately disappointing. Also pension income is taxable, and you do not know what the tax regime will be when you start drawing it. Nor do you know how much you will get, unless you are among the fortunate employees in a guaranteed final salary scheme (see below). With a personal pension, income will depend on the growth of your fund and the prevailing annuity rates.

So do take the time to consider carefully whether a conventional pension is the best option for you, or whether you might not be better off investing for your retirement via alternatives, such as Maxi-ISAs, investment property and directly owned shares or equity funds (see below).

Most of us have two pensions, one from the state and another from our employer, or, if self-employed, in the form of a personal pension plan. But present savings levels are lamentably low and will not provide most of us with the income we expect and need to maintain our standard of living when we retire. Unless we take the initiative now, while we are earning, to invest the maximum to create wealth, we shall be among the many who, according to the Government, will be one third underfunded when they retire.

State pension

Your state pension depends on your national insurance contributions (NICs) throughout your working life. Everyone with an earnings record gets a basic state pension. But do not hold your breadth over how much you will get. It is constantly being eroded and the eligibility rules are not written in stone. You can find out what state pension you are projected to receive by completing a BR 19 form, available from your local DSS office.

Company pensions

These come in two varieties:

• Non-contributory: 100 per cent paid by the employer.

- Contributory: typically 5–6 per cent of salary is deducted by employers from your pay: the maximum you can contribute is 15 per cent per annum.

You can make up the maximum allowed, and thus boost your benefit by paying:

- Additional Voluntary Contributions (AVC); or
- Free Standing Additional Voluntary Contributions (FSAVC).

What are the tax benefits of these company pensions?
- In exempt approved schemes employees do not pay tax on their employer's contributions, subject to an earnings cap (£90,600 in 1999/2000).
- Tax relief at the employee's highest marginal rate on his/her contribution.

Who is eligible for a company pension?
- That is up to the employer, although sex discrimination is not allowed.
- Generally decided according to age and length of service.
- Not the self-employed, but they retain pension rights from any previous company schemes when they leave employed work.

Types of company pension:
- In a defined *benefit* scheme, the investment risk is borne by the employer, not the employee. The benefit is guaranteed (i.e. it is a fixed percentage of final salary – the maximum is two thirds).
- In a defined *contribution* scheme, the investment risk is borne by the employee, not the employer. The cost to employers is known (i.e. a fixed annual contribution) but the future benefits are not. This type of company pension is also known as a money-purchase scheme.
- In a group personal pension (money-purchase) the investment risk is borne by the employee, not the employer. It allows the same maximum contribution according to your age as with a personal pension (see below). You and your employer can put in a combined maximum of 17.5 per cent of your annual gross earnings until you are thirty-five and that rises to 40 per cent for the over-sixties.
- A stakeholder pension (available from April 2001) is a low-cost flexible alternative to company pension plans or to personal pensions. It is aimed at those earning from £9,000 to £18,500. Employers who do not now offer a pension scheme will be obliged to introduce it. The cost will be capped to a no frills (no advice?) fee of 1 per cent or so of the value of the fund with

no extra charges for transfers. Maximum allowed contributions will be £3,600 a year.

What happens to the pension fund of an employee leaving their employer?

- You retain your entitlement, which will be protected to a large extent against inflation.
- Alternatively, the retained benefits can be transferred into the pension scheme of your new employer, or into a personal pension.
- But beware of transfer into a personal pension. You may be giving up a guaranteed pension for life from your former employer and taking all the investment risk yourself.

A company pension is deferred pay to which you are entitled. So take the time to study your scheme booklet and understand what you can expect to receive (see Step 1). A defined benefit company scheme, particularly of the non-contributory variety, is a win-win proposition. All the investment risk is borne by your employer, and you receive a guaranteed annual pension from when you retire until you die. The best defined benefit schemes offer:

- Two thirds of final salary after a maximum of forty years employment.
- Pension based on total earnings not just basic pay.
- Death-in-retirement pension for your partner (two-thirds your own) and pension/s for dependent children.
- Death-in-service pension for partner and children and lump sum of up to four times annual salary.
- If you change jobs, your pension is preserved and grows in line with inflation.

Such generous company pensions can be poisoned chalices. Academic research shows that highly paid men aged 45–49 with defined benefit pensions are more likely to be fired before they detonate a time-bomb in pensions costs for their employers, after the age of fifty.[2] Increasingly, companies are switching from defined benefit to defined contribution (money-purchase) schemes. The latter in no way, however, guarantee sufficient pension income for life. But those employees with defined

[2] *The Decline of Employment Among Older People in Britain*, published in January 1999 by the Centre for Analysis of Social Exclusion at the London School of Economics.

benefit schemes who are 'coaxed' into early retirement may still be better off as their pensions can be enhanced to make it worth their while to retire early, and they would still have a guaranteed level of income.

Increasingly, governments and companies cop out of defined benefits pension arrangements and encourage us to take out money-purchase pension schemes. If you are offered a defined benefit pension you should grab it. But money-purchase company pensions are not quite so compelling.

Personal pensions

The allure of personal pensions is essentially tax driven. They are suitable for self-employed people or employees who are not in occupational pension schemes. Personal pensions provide retirement benefits from the age of fifty to seventy-five and are funded by payment of single or regular premiums. As discussed earlier, the former have lower charges than the latter (see also disadvantages overleaf).

Advantages
- Tax relief at your highest marginal rate.
- The fund grows tax-free, although dividend income has effectively been reduced by 20 per cent. That is because pension funds can no longer reclaim the tax credit.
- Carry-back/carry-forward provisions let you use past allowances over a period of up to seven years to make maximum use of the tax relief to which you are entitled.
- You can put the whole fund into a wide range of investments, especially through self-invested personal pensions which can include directly held shares and investment property. These are most suitable once you have built up a six-figure fund.
- You can and should take the maximum 25 per cent tax-free out of your pension pot on retirement.
- If you die before you reach the age of seventy-five, and have not yet bought an an-nuity, or taken any income out of your pension pot, it can pass down to beneficiaries free of IHT provided it is written in trust and therefore does not become part of your estate.
- You can put off buying your annuity until you are seventy-five.
- You can go on working after you have drawn benefits.

- Your policy is your own property.
- You may borrow against your accumulated fund or the projected lump sum benefit at your retirement.

Disadvantages

- Contributions ranking for tax relief are limited to 17.5 per cent of earnings until you are thirty-five, rising to 40 per cent for the over-sixties up to the earnings cap.
- Charges can be heavy, particularly for regular premium policies in early years when costs of setting up the plan and sales commissions are deducted.
- Loss of flexibility just as you get stiff in the bones. Unless the Government changes the rules, you are obliged to use 75 per cent of the savings in your personal pension fund to buy an annuity by the time you are seventy-five.
- While that is a guaranteed income for life it also guarantees loss of capital with no savings left to pass on to children.
- Annuities can provide spouses with pensions and guarantees for up to ten years – at the expense of your initial income.
- Annuity rates shadow the yield from government gilts. When these are low, annuity rates are distinctly unalluring.
- With personal pensions you are stuck with buying an annuity at some stage unless you die before the age of seventy-five.

Annuities – income for life but not perpetual

Compulsory purchase annuities come in many varieties to provide a fixed, escalating or variable income for life. They can be guaranteed for up to ten years but eventually the guarantee runs out. Annuities are not allowed to be perpetual, and passed down through the generations. They are designed to give you an income in your retirement, however long you live – they are therefore a form of insurance against long life. As you get older, and your life expectancy is shortened, so you would get a higher rate of annuity. But how long you can afford to wait before you buy an annuity depends on whether you have sufficient other sources of income when you retire. But why would you really want to deplete wealth that you can, in all instances, pass down to future generations by purchasing an annuity?

Income drawdown now – but pay later?

If you choose to delay the purchase of an annuity, and keep your pension pot invested, you are allowed in the meantime to take income out equivalent to between 35 and 100 per cent of what you would get from an ordinary annuity at the time. This is called **income drawdown**. You are only allowed to take out a tax-free cash lump sum of up to 25 per cent at the time you commence income drawdown. But unless your remaining funds are invested purely in shares, you risk eroding the capital in your pot. Consequently your fund would shrink and you may have less with which to buy an annuity later – and end up with less income than you would have had at the beginning.

That is because annuity rates are always slightly higher than gilt yields due to the mortality element of an annuity. That is to say, if you live longer than average, you will profit from those not so fortunate and vice versa. If your pension were partly invested in cash, gilts and property, it would be unlikely to produce enough to to pay an income, pay the costs of running the plan, and keep up your fund size. So income drawdown would not improve your income. It can be better than an annuity on death, but only if you die before buying an annuity. It is a gamble that annuity rates will improve but that is by no means certain or even probable as long as inflation and government borrowings remain low.

Recent changes mean that income drawdown may also be available to those with company pensions. Find out your own options, but the above issues still apply.

Costs

Tax benefits in personal pensions are all very well, but they do not always make up for the disadvantages and risks described above. As already stressed, the costs and inflexibility of some pension products are prohibitive. Moreover the negative impact of costs is exacerbated by frequent job mobility.

Inflation risk in personal pensions

When you are young, what rate you will get for an annuity when you retire, or what is the capital risk within your pension fund should not concern you. Your risk is inflation. The only sure way you will beat inflation in fifteen, twenty or twenty-five years is to invest now in equity funds. If you take too little risk with your pension savings you cannot be sure to outpace inflation in the long term. Managed funds or with-profit funds may not expose you enough to capital growth through shares – the best protection against risk of inflation.

While you are young and employed it is hard to imagine a time when you can no longer earn a good living. But that time may come sooner than you think. Old age in western society is defined by retirement and pension systems. In the UK, the state pension age is sixty-five for men and sixty for women (to be raised to sixty-five for those retiring after 2020). But technological and other innovations have increased productivity and prosperity and cut the length of our working lives.

We reach our earnings peak younger and younger, while our life expectancy is now much longer. Policy-makers throughout the western world have not adjusted to the reality that people could easily live well into their eighties or nineties but that their productive life may end in their early fifties. How do you fund thirty or forty years of living without earned income? You invest now to grow capital and produce income while in retirement, whenever that may be, and for however long you may live. To become financially self-reliant is to relieve the State and your family and friends of the burden of your future welfare. It is a noble pursuit that is also hugely enjoyable and life-enhancing.

Some of you may choose to retire early to enjoy increased prosperity in the form of increased leisure. But many more of us will be 'offered' early retirement: not an offer we can refuse. Unless we have relevant skills (in IT for example) or are well established at the top of our professions or careers, we may be forced out of employment long before the usual retirement age. So whatever your age, if you have not got some form of pension, other than the pittance you will get from the State, then a pension is a '**1**' priority.

Alternative pensions

You need not necessarily take up a formal personal pension. You could instead:

- Build up and manage your own 'pension fund' via regular savings in unit trusts, investment trusts and directly held shares. You would lose out on tax relief you would get on contributions to a personal pension plan. But you would retain control over all your capital for life. And you still have your annual capital gains exemption (£7,100 in 1999/2000) to mitigate your tax.
- Tuck away the maximum allowed for you and your spouse each year in tax-sheltered wrappers such as Maxi-ISAs.
- Buy-to-rent property and/or plan to sell/downscale your main residence when you retire.

The UK Government, like that of the US, has proffered various tax shelters to encourage people to save. The Personal Equity Plan (PEP) was introduced by Margaret Thatcher's Conservative government in 1987 but killed off by Tony Blair's New Labour in 1999/2000, and replaced on 6 April 1999 by the less generous ISA, a hybrid of the PEP and the now extinct TESSA.

PEPs were designed to encourage greater share ownership among private investors. Privatisations of British Gas, British Petroleum and British Telecom had already been widely taken up by the general public – at a profit. At first, the maximum you were allowed to invest via a PEP in equity and income funds, or directly held shares and bonds, was £2,400. But by 1990, that limit had increased to £6,000 and in 1992 to £9,000. PEPs ignited explosive growth in retail financial services. Unit trusts in shares or fixed-income and tracker funds were snapped up by PEP holders. Even directly held shares could be sheltered within a PEP.

The TESSA was popular with new investors looking for tax-free income. It allowed you to put up to £9,000 into a bank or building society over five years and let the interest accumulate tax-free. Existing PEPs and TESSAs taken out before 6 April 1999 remain potent investments for capital and income growth.

The maximum investment allowed in the ISA is £7,000 in 1999/2000 and £5,000 thereafter. The ISA is a tax-free wrapper for shares, bonds, limited amounts of cash and life insurance. Mr Blair's government has guaranteed its tax-free status for ten years, and although no-one can guarantee his government's longevity, the promotion of personal savings, as part of welfare reform, would appear to be on an all-party agenda, not just in the UK but in all developed economies.

Get a mortgage

Apart from pension planning, the other major piece in your personal wealth plan is likely to be your mortgage. There is acute competition for your business, as new lenders, with the latest technology and without costly high street branches enter the field. A sizeable but manageable mortgage will impose a regular savings discipline while also allowing you to leverage a small capital base (your deposit) into a larger capital asset (the property).

Mortgages on residential property are either:
- Capital and interest or repayment loans.
- Interest-only loans.

The repayment loan mortgage

This is very profitable for the lender, assuming low inflation. That is because the debt is reduced (amortised) very slowly – typically over 25 years – and the lender charges interest at a variable rate over all that time, compounding his profit. A repayment mortgage guarantees to pay back the entire loan plus interest in equal monthly payments which fluctuate according to interest rates. At the start, most of the monthly repayments will be made up of interest – because the outstanding loan is still great. But as the debt is gradually reduced, you would pay more in capital repayment each month.

The advantage of this type of mortgage from a borrower's point of view is that, provided monthly repayments are kept up, the loan and interest will be repaid in full by the end of the term. It is also easier to budget, subject to changes in interest rates that in turn affect the monthly repayments.

The interest-only mortgage

This involves paying interest on the entire loan throughout the duration of the agreement, and repaying the debt in full at term. There are many variations in this type of mortgage including **variable**, **fixed interest**, **capped and collared**, **discounted**, and **deferred interest** mortgages. There is an increasing array of new and exciting mortgage offers. Use the Internet for the latest information and look for lenders that offer the greatest flexibility with fewest strings attached in the form of imposition of tied products, such as insurance, into the deal. Or you can go to a top mortgage broker. Better still, go to two and compare their offers. They charge from 0.3 to 1 per cent of the loan. The best brokers will save you the sum of their fee and a lot of leg work. They should identify the most suitable mortgage deal for you and be able to project forward the schedule of repayments, and costs/penalties should you repay the loan early. In Step 4, on owning property, you will find a checklist of what to watch out for in a commercial property loan agreement.

Rent-a-room to boost income

Once you have your mortgage, one way to raise extra income, possibly towards paying for it or alternatively to boost your finances in retirement, is to rent-a-room in your home. The rent-a-room rules exempt you from income tax if your gross rental receipts (that is before expenses) are £4,250 or less. But you cannot then claim any of the expenses of letting against your tax. Rents received over the £4,250 exemption limit can be taxed on an alternative basis to produce a lower tax bill. You can opt either:

A. To pay tax on the profit you make from letting, worked out in the normal way for a rental business – that is rent received less expenses.
or
B. To pay tax on the gross amount of your receipts (including receipts for any related services such as laundry and meals) less the £4,250 exemption limit.

You can calculate which formula would suit you better. Use the following example to help you.

Example – rent-a-room

Joe lets out a room in his home for £100 a week, so his gross receipts are £5,200 a year. His expenses are £700 a year and so his net profit is therefore £4,500. His tax-free exemption is £4,250 so the excess of Joe's receipts over his exemption is £950 (£5,200 less £4,250).
If he opted for:

Plan A he would pay tax on his actual net profit of £4,500.
Plan B he would pay tax on a profit of £950.

But Sarah rents a room in her house and collects a total rent of £5,400. She has expenses of £4,500, so her net profit is £900. The excess of her gross receipts over the £4,250 exemption is £1,150 (£5,400 less £4,250).
If she opted for:

Plan A she would pay tax on £900.
Plan B she would pay tax on £1,150.

Those are the broad investment options. You will want to look further into each to identify which are right for you. Don't cut corners when making your inquiries before you invest. Private investors will often take advice on money matters from colleagues or friends while casually standing at the office coffee machine or at a dinner party or on the golf course. But free advice is invariably not worth the paper it is *not* printed on. Personally, I love advising myself on how to manage my money, and I enjoy the homework involved.

What the professionals can do for you

Under the Financial Services Act 1986, all investment advisers must be authorised to sell products or give advice, whether it be to professional investors or to members of the public. He or she must send you a terms of business letter which spells out the 'key facts' of any contract that they may enter with you. The letter must state clearly whether the financial adviser is a 'tied' agent – i.e. a company representative able to sell only the products/services of one provider – or whether they are 'independent'. They may not be both under the 'polarisation' rules introduced in 1986.

Yet in mid-summer 1999, the Office of Fair Trading proposed to relax these polarisation rules regarding the sale of collective investments via IFAs. That would allow so called 'independent' financial advisers effectively to become agents for any given providers of unit trusts, investment trusts and oeics. The OFT argued its proposals – subject to approval by the Chancellor of the Exchequer – would increase competition while critics protested that the boundary between what is truly independent financial advice and what is not, would, as a result, become even more blurred.

The polarisation rules would still prevail regarding the sale of life assurance products such as endowments, with-profits bonds, and pensions under the OFT proposals. But the fiercely competitive providers of collective funds would be free to recruit (not so) independent financial advisers to help market their funds as 'brands' in financial services. The danger is that some IFAs might be tempted to recommend unsuitable products for self-serving reasons.

Now independent financial advisers have a legal duty to recommend the most suitable products with regard to your needs, circumstances and what is available in the market – and the best among them do just that. Otherwise they are effectively mis-selling. A good IFA will design a bespoke long term investment plan to help you reach your goals, and he/she will also recommend products or services that suit your needs.

But clearly, the designation 'independent' financial adviser is a misnomer – and always has been. Most IFAs already derive substantial commissions from providers of the products and services they sell to you –

even when they are not tied agents. So insist on an adviser who charges hourly fees and does not take sales commissions so there is no incentive for him or her to sell you the products that pay the highest commissions.

Get the terms, and a client agreement letter before you deal

Before any work is done, professional firms must issue a client agreement letter of engagement that explains in detail what the adviser will do for you. Then you will be asked to provide accurate information for a fact find so that your adviser can go through the necessary preparation detailed in Steps 1 and 2 and write a plan that is appropriate to your needs. Make sure you get a copy of the fact find and check that it is accurate. The adviser must send you a 'reason why' letter explaining the rationale of any recommendations. Read this carefully. Make sure you understand it and do not be afraid to challenge your financial adviser. If in doubt get a second opinion on it, even if it means paying another professional. Then keep the recommendation on file.

Compile a fact-find of your own – on the adviser

The key questions to ask him or her are:
- How is your firm regulated and is it independent or a tied agent?
- What activities is the firm authorised, and as important, not authorised, to carry out?
- What experience/academic/professional qualifications do you have?
- In what areas of financial planning do you specialise?
- How long have you been with this firm/advising clients?
- How many clients do you have? How long have you acted for most?
- May I contact any of your clients for a reference?
- Are you personally registered, and if so, with which authority?
- What is your investment philosophy and your approach to financial planning?
- What is the best/worst result you ever achieved?
- How much are, and how will I pay for, your services?

- If I buy a product you recommend that pays commission, how will that money be treated?
- Is any part of your salary/compensation based on selling products?
- Would you have any conflicts of interest in acting for me?
- Can you please spell out these points clearly in your client agreement letter?

Your fee-based adviser must put in writing how the commissions will be treated. You should in most cases expect effectively to share sales commissions by agreeing that they will be offset against the firm's advisory fees or re-invested in your plan. If you prefer not to pay fees, then you will pay indirectly via sales commissions on products you buy via your adviser. Ask him/her to put in writing how much commission he or she will make.

Check that the IFA is indeed registered, and authorised to give you financial advice. Probe their qualifications. They are required to pass basic exams for the Investment Advice Certificate (IAC) or the Financial Planning Certificate (FPC), while most stockbrokers must pass the Registered Persons exam before they are allowed to give advice on individual shares. But why not go for an adviser who has passed tougher tests, such as the Advanced Financial Planning Certificate (AFPC); the Institute of Financial Planning's fellowship exams, or for shares, the Securities Institute's diploma qualifications?

Some solicitors and accountants have also entered the lucrative field of investment advice through fully integrated IFA services. They are well placed, as trusted advisers with knowledge of their clients' finances, to sell them financial products and services related to tax planning such as taking out life insurance to mitigate against inheritance tax or investing in a personal pension to obtain maximum income tax relief, or to give trust management. But your accountant or solicitor, acting as a financial adviser, must also declare commissions from product sales to you. You could then deal over sharing these kick-backs via rebates, or a credit note.

Depending on your needs you may not want a financial planner, but an investment adviser, who helps you construct your own investment portfolio of directly held shares. However, unless you have a reasonable sum to invest you should opt for pooled investments such as unit and investment trusts where your purchasing power will go further until you have built up enough fire power to build your own share portfolio. You can start when you have enough capital to put a minimum of £3,000 into at least eight shares with opposite risks. Do not wait until you have the full £24,000 plus: you can move into directly held shares gradually as you build up your savings.

Investment managers

These will normally have complete discretion over the management of your money. But as already noted, unless you have substantial funds to invest, you will invariably be herded into managed funds and will be not be allowed to pick what to buy or sell, or when to do so. You would only be able to select the type of managed funds in which you want to invest. You may pay dealing commissions and annual management fees, based on the value of your investments, to either an investment manager or private bank or advisory stockbroker offering private client portfolio management. Incentive fees, based on the profits the manager makes in your account, work best – but usually only apply to large portfolios.

Personal investment advisers

With a personal investment adviser you will retain control over your investment decisions and draw on your adviser's research, experience and opinion before deciding what shares to buy or sell, or indeed how much to put into shares, as opposed to fixed income investments or cash. Some advisory stockbrokers are excellent at synthesising information relevant to you so that you can make sound, common sense decisions about how to invest your own money. Others push the house line (put out by their research departments or investment committees).

Execution-only stockbrokers

If, like me, you want to make your own investment decisions (mistakes and all) go to an execution-only stockbroker for shares. Such brokers will take your (unsolicited) orders and execute them. You can also deal online if you are confident you know what you are doing but do not sacrifice adequate service, and/or sound advice and excellent execution for a few pounds of saved commission. Be vigilant when dealing online. According to the venerable Washington-based Securities and Exchange Commission (SEC) – an independent agency of the US Government with statutory powers to regulate the securities industry – online investing has given con-artists a new way to cheat investors.

The SEC recommends that before you invest, you always obtain written financial information, such as a prospectus or annual report, offering circular and financial statements. Compare the written information with what you have read online. But if you are told no such information is available, it is safe to turn off your computer. You could otherwise be involved in a fraud.

The competition for your money is intense and will increasingly force providers to cut their charges and add value to their products and services. This is a buyer's market. So shop around.

Step 4

Own Property: Be a Landlord

Put your money out to work over the long term and collect rent from property that will enhance your wealth

STEP 4
Own Property: Be a Landlord

In Step 4, we look at property, whether commercial or residential, as an investment for rental income and capital growth. Your home does not count as pure investment because you derive no income from it. On the contrary, your home is a consumer product that costs you money to buy, to improve, to repair, to maintain and to finance. Only if you sell it for a profit (usually tax-free) and move into another that costs less, will you reap a profit from the roof over your head. But you can plan ahead to sell it and scale down, and thus turn your home it into a tax-free 'pension'.

Some of you perhaps know the basics described in Step 3 and anyway may prefer to own property which you can touch, see and use, rather than just hold securities with only pieces of paper to show for it. You might not like having to tolerate stock market volatility and so take comfort from property, as it is not priced every second of every trading day on capital markets as securities are. But do not delude yourself that property is 'as safe as houses'. Your profit depends on the location of your property, the timing of your purchase, inflation, cost of money and planning controls. These factors will determine growth of rental income and the capital value of your property over several years.

Property values and yields can be highly volatile. The market can become over-supplied, and/or over-bought or hit by legislative/political interference. In such circumstances, property prices can fall. You would lose money if you failed to identify and measure your risks in the context of your strategy, and to secure reasonable long term finance to give you staying power.

Property is land with a physical structure on it that can be put to use, and therefore generates income. Traditionally, property has been a respected and well recognised store of wealth. The rental income from agricultural and commercial property was, until securities markets were invented, the only means of deriving a 'dividend' from asset backed investments. Commercial property can have bond-type characteristics when let on long leases to reliable tenants, providing secure income. Rental income also represents the dividend from let residential property, whether furnished or unfurnished.

Rental dividend from investment property is commonly used to pay the interest on loans raised to buy it and to pay down the debt. When your gross annual rental income covers the annual cost of the property loan and all other outgoings, the property investment is said to 'wash its face'. That is the benchmark you should normally apply before you buy. But property should be only a part of your long term wealth plan: it is too illiquid an investment to carry all your life savings.

Property v. personal pensions

The magic of **gearing** (borrowing) in property may not be as beguiling at first sight as the tax relief from investment in a personal pension. But the allure of gearing is quite compelling. Take a higher rate tax payer who invests a single premium of £120,000 net of 40 per cent tax relief, into a personal pension: he would immediately have a gross fund of £200,000. That year, he also puts another £120,000 into a 25 per cent deposit on a commercial property worth £480,000 and borrows the remaining £360,000 to buy it. Assuming both the pension and the property grew at an average 10 per cent compound a year, his pension would be worth £400,000 and the property £960,000 in just over seven years, when, let us say, he retires.

He could take 25 per cent in cash out of his pension fund tax-free, but unless the Government changes the rules, he would have to buy an annuity with the remaining 75 per cent compound by the time he is seventy-five. On the other hand, his property, if sold, the loan repaid and the capital gains tax paid, would still leave him with a lump sum in excess of his pension fund. Or he could choose to keep it and enjoy rental income possibly higher than an annuity. His property would have provided him with a 'pension' which if not geared to the extent of 40 per cent tax relief, is, however, geared to 75 per cent bank borrowings – which in turn are tax deductible. He would also retain control over the capital invested in his 'property pension' throughout his life and could pass it on when he dies. But his pension pot would be lost at his death – unless he died before reaching seventy-five or had not yet bought an annuity, nor drawn income from his pension, and had also written his pension in trust for his beneficiaries. Of course, if he could put his investment property into a self-invested pension scheme, he would benefit from the leverage of borrowing *and* the tax relief.

Property investment is not an amateur sport. You are up against the pros and so must be highly professional. You cannot accurately assess potential profit/costs until you have first minutely studied the specific market in the type, size and quality of property you seek. Even when demand for rental is less buoyant, your returns should be satisfactory when compared with those from cash, bonds and shares. That assumes you have bought your property for a reasonable price, having worked out meticulously the potential rental income from it, and the future re-letting risk. In short, you must manage your investment property efficiently.

Homework – and legwork

Whatever property you buy, first do your **due diligence**: that involves homework and legwork. The work does not stop with your purchase. When you own property, it is largely up to you, or your agent, to make your asset sweat. Investment in property is effectively an active rental or trading business. You have to be hands-on in managing it. You can create value by intelligent management of good property, but third rate locations or buildings with structural problems that require specialist knowledge are best left to professionals. Their high potential rewards would be your high potential risks.

You will not be able to beat a general decline in property values and/or rental income any more than you can influence share prices. But you can, and must, pick at least a good secondary location in commercial property. In the residential field, even if you buy the worst house in the best street, you would have a better quality investment, which would be easier to finance, to market and eventually to sell. If you are disciplined and buy property for a reasonable price, sensibly financed, you will reduce your risks of capital loss in a downturn and enjoy a good rental yield.

There are two main tenures when you own property.

- Freehold: you own it outright and are known as the landlord.
- Leasehold: you hold the property on a lease for a fixed number of years.

The adage in the property market is that only three things matter: *location, location, location*. Certainly location is critical in residential property. With commercial property, dependability of the tenant is also important. But if you have to choose, go for location.

The least sexy characteristic of property, be it commercial or residential, is its lack of liquidity. Property is expensive to buy and to sell, with stamp duty, solicitors' and surveyors' fees payable. It is sometimes hard to sell when you want to, even in buoyant market conditions. But lack of liquidity imposes discipline to make sure you are conservative in your assumptions of income/re-letting risk and the cost of maintenance, repairs, voids and taxes. You will make money from property if you are strict in managing the finances so as to maintain positive cash flow while you hold it.

It can take several weeks, if not months, to put the property up for sale, show it to prospective buyers, agree its sale and receive the proceeds – that is the cash. In a bad market, you might not sell your property for a long time, unless you let it go at a fire sale price – which defeats the purpose of your investment. But you ought not to find yourself forced to sell if, before you buy, you do your due diligence well.

Indirect investment in property

If you want to invest in residential property but take a smaller stake in commercial property, you could buy shares of blue chip commercial property companies, either directly or through a unit trust or property funds managed by insurance companies. Or, buy shares in surrogate property companies such as hotel groups (as long as they mainly own their freeholds) or a conservatively financed stores group. For example, Marks & Spencer in the spring of 1999 retained some of the best freehold and long leasehold store sites in the UK. You would buy shares in such surrogates not just for their trading profits, but also their potential **break-up value**.

Shares in the likes of M&S would normally carry a premium for the quality, potential growth and goodwill of its business. Its property portfolio would also command premium values. M&S stores are on prime sites where other retailers cluster. All the same, shares in M&S, or some such other surrogate property business, could prove a better investment than shares or funds in pure property companies – which woefully underperformed in the 1995/8 bull market. This is not least because if a property-rich trading company, such as M&S, failed to derive a satisfactory return on its assets, sooner or later it would be taken over – with its own money. That is to say the assets of the business would be used to raise the loans to mount a leveraged break-up takeover bid for it, which is effectively what Granada did when it mounted a leveraged £3.5 billion hostile takeover bid for Forte in late 1995. Granada was able to carve £1.6 billion out of Forte by selling off some of its assets. By 1999, Granada had reduced its debt to buy Forte to some £1.8 billion.

One reason for UK property companies' underperformance is the market's innate dislike of capital intensive businesses with slow/low return on capital employed. Another is caution. The companies' shares are invariably at a discount to their stated **net asset value** (NAV). Finally, the directors' annual remuneration/management costs are high when compared with the capital profits realised and distributed via dividends to shareholders. So dividend income is low from property shares compared with the rents you would derive from direct personal investment in property.

In property, timing is everything

In property, timing is all. Make hay while the sun shines. But when there is a chill in the air, because interest rates are relatively high, you will find good opportunities to buy for capital growth. Property yields rise when capital values fall right across the board in a general property slump. That is when, ideally, you should strike as an investor. You cannot always choose when you buy your own home, but with investment, be disciplined. Timing the property market is easier than trying to time the stock market. That is because the share and bond markets are highly liquid and the ebb and flow of capital into securities is hard to predict in the short term.

But **fundamentals** drive property up or down. Favourable supply/demand leads to positive cash flow, and profit. In that sunny climate, investor/lender confidence grows regarding re-letting risk, future cost of borrowings and future inflation. Given investor confidence property will boom, even when interest rates are relatively high in real terms. But watch out for over-confidence (greed) on the part of investors and lenders. Over-supply, over-valuation and aggressive lending on unrealistic growth expectations create a bubble that eventually bursts.

The golden rule for capital growth

The golden rule is to buy property when interest rates are higher than property yields but the cost of money is falling. Sell property when the cost of money is lower than property yields, but set to rise. That may sound illogical, in view of the relative ease with which you can raise loans when money is cheap. But for high capital growth, at tolerable risk, do not run with the herd into property. Instead, bide your time and enter the field when high interest rates have depressed business activity and tenant demand is lower. You will then be able to buy property at reasonable prices and enjoy growth in future rental income and capital value. The cycle usually takes five years or more; certainly do not even consider buying property if your time frame is less.

Trading property for a quick 'turn'

Sometimes you can buy a property for less than its market value in a 'fire sale' for example, or because it has a reversionary lease, or needs extensive refurbishment. If you are confident that you can make a good profit from buying it in order to 'turn it', then go ahead. But short term trading in investment property is not generally recommended. The costs of entry into, and exit from, property are high. You would have to clear at least 10 per cent before you covered your costs. You would also be up against astute professional traders. They may well know more than you about any problems associated with the 'bargain' and which have reduced its value.

Exceptional trading opportunities, prudently assessed and well financed, should be seized. But otherwise do not try to compete against professional traders. Where there are 'pros' you will inevitably come up against 'cons'. Instead, plan your finances so as to buy-and-hold the best property you can afford for many years and you should make a substantial profit while deriving a good income.

At auction

In early 1999, when the cost of money in the UK was some 7 per cent and forecast to fall towards 3.5 per cent Euro rates, London property auctions, whether for commercial or residential, were packed with up to 750 eager investors (and not a few dealers) at a time. Amid the excitement, disingenuous investors, lured by high yields, bought property straight off the catalogue. It is mailed out about three to four weeks before the event and forms a contract for sale. The particulars embrace pertinent information, i.e. for commercial property, the terms of the lease, tenancies, rent reviews and so on. Location is shown by a street map and a photograph.

Prospective buyers have time to view sites, and if you are one, you would be well advised not just to visit the property, but also to ask nosey questions at the local agents and check out the planning, parking, rubbish collection, shopping and travel amenities in the area. The local planning officer will show you pending planning applications and tell you which have been accepted or refused recently. Stand outside any shop you plan to buy and count the 'foot fall' in the street. But most important of all, check out what property men call the 'legals'. That is, ask your solicitor to examine the conditions of sale and the titles of the property, including leases to tenants, and any other relevant points.

Check out the legals – or legally, you end up paying for... nothing

By checking out the legals you may discover facts that are not in the auctioneer's glossy brochure. Also be ready to pay for an independent valuation or a desktop valuation as the basis for a loan. Before an auction, lenders will give you only indicative terms, subject to valuation/authorisation. Lenders are not bound to honour these terms. If you have not done your homework thoroughly before you buy at auction, and the lender backs away because of problems with the structure or lease, you will either have to find alternative financing or the site will be resold, and you will lose your 10 per cent deposit – and could be sued for full cost!

The top twenty UK auctioneers brought down the hammer on some 21,000 UK properties in 1998. Auctions were once perceived as the dumping ground for virtually unsaleable properties with problems such as structural settlement, legal defects, sitting tenants and the like. But now they are an efficient market, where buyers can bid on a wide choice of property (including some dogs), and sellers attain a greater audience – particularly now via the Internet.

Beginners beware of auctions

Before graduating to making bids at a property auction, attend several to get a feel for the market. Try 'dry buying': that is, note down virtual bids on properties you have researched and would want to own, and compare them with real prices fetched. Keep it virtual until your 'bids' correspond closely with reality. Even if you cannot attend many auctions, you can obtain results from the auctioneers – or read the auction results weekly in *Estates Gazette*.

When you are ready to make an actual bid, go into the auction prepared, with a reasonable walk-away limit in your head. Once that limit is breached, move out of the room, or you may get carried away as crowd psychology can be pervasive and dangerous (see Step 7). The auctioneer conjures up high bids by stoking up excitement in the room: if you feel a rush, you had best rush out of the door. Conversely, when an auction is under-attended, and bids hard to extract, fear might stop you from buying a good property. You could just put in a postal bid and not attend the auction.

At the fall of the auctioneer's gavel, a binding contract is effected. If you are the successful bidder you must provide your particulars and those of your solicitor and pay a 10 per cent deposit to the auctioneer, acting as stakeholder. Contracts are exchanged and completion – payment of the balance of the purchase price – usually takes place after 28 days. Sellers pay auctioneers 1.5–2.5 per cent of proceeds, depending on the property, and some £400–1,000 for an insert in their catalogues. Buyers pay no commissions or price of entry.

Buy right to produce positive cash flow

Capital gain from property, fuelled by inflation, has been almost a foregone conclusion since the war. But now, with low inflation, you have to buy right and juggle debt to produce positive cash flow to make money from property. The cash flow from rent is attractive – and you would collect it in advance but pay interest on loans in arrears.

The fiscal culture that has encouraged homeowners to take on big mortgages is now changing in the UK. But the British, even those in their twenties, remain psychologically inclined to buy their own homes rather than rent them, as the French and Germans do. That is because for generations our homes were our only store of real wealth, and we 'invested' by paying off mortgages.

Traditionally, inflation ensured that profit from property purchases funded by borrowings was almost inevitable. The general view was that UK property was the safest possible investment – the worst that could happen was that a couple of tiles could fall off the roof. But in 1974 there was a property crash, triggered by reckless over-lending by secondary banks. They made loans secured on vacant land that did not yield income.

As building costs soared, through inflation, the value of the land crashed and developers could not pay interest on their bank loans. The banks called in the loans, and that meant massive selling of land, which further depressed values. Only developers with sufficient income from let property or some other business survived. Investors may have taken a hit from increasing variable interest rates, but if their property produced sufficient income, they were protected, as were their lenders.

Developer Gerald Ronson of Heron International, for example, had a chain of petrol stations that pumped out the cash flow to service his property loans throughout the 1974/5 UK property crash, and so kept his bankers at bay. But in the early 1990s, Heron had grown massively and was highly leveraged. Heron had a first class portfolio of office and leisure property in the UK and in Europe, but faltered over an investment in the savings and loan industry in the US. Ronson's petrol pumps could no longer service Heron's loans and his bankers agreed to swap debt for equity. They had little choice. To pull the rug from such a substantial enterprise would have been to crystallise around £1 billion of losses.

As Onassis once advised, 'borrow billions and the banks are at your beck and call'. But do not rely on Onassis' advice when servicing your bank loan and paying it down. Make sure you have positive cash flow.

The UK stock market plunged in 1974. It was a great shock to property owners and shareholders alike. There was a short, violent recession, concentrated mainly in the property market, which pervaded all trading businesses. A miserable period followed, when Prime Minister

Ted Heath put Britain on a three-day week. But by 1975/6, recovery was underway and it accelerated after Margaret Thatcher was elected in 1979. The UK, under Thatcher, would come to be perceived by overseas investors as an enterprise culture.

But in 1982, there was a hard recession. The property market took off between 1984 and 1989 when fortunes were made from trading in property. Taxes fell to a maximum 40 per cent for the highest rate income tax, capital gains tax and inheritance tax. Lawyer David Brecher, veteran of multi-billion-pound commercial property deals recalls, 'Property investors regarded it almost a pleasure to pay only 40 per cent tax on their profit.'

During the depths of recession in 1992, when interest rates reached some 15 per cent, beleaguered UK property developers used to cheer themselves up by chanting a mantra: 'Stay alive until '95; go to heaven in '97.' They were spot on: property did recover substantially by 1997, along with the economy and the stock market, and office rents in the City, by 1999, fully regained the peaks they reached in the late 80s.

The tax angle in buying-to-rent residential/commercial property

A succession of UK governments have tried to make residential property investment attractive in order to revive the private rented sector in the UK, with tax breaks for investors in property, whether residential or commercial. First, unlike with share investment, you can deduct the total cost of the interest on the loan raised to buy your property against your gross rental income. Then all the running expenses – such as ground rent/council tax, insurance, repairs/maintenance, legal/professional fees, agents' fees and/or cost of advertising – are also tax deductible. Finally, capital expenses such as refurbishment, extensions and structural work that constitute improvements can be deducted from your capital gain on the sale of the property.

These tax breaks allow you to use tax-subsidised finance to grow a large capital asset from a small capital base. You also enjoy income net of expenses (but before tax). Finally, when you sell it you will pay less capital gains tax on your profit by deducting what you spent to add value. The Inland Revenue's guide[3] is a must-read for all would-be landlords, including those who wish to own property abroad.

More tax-efficient to own property personally or in a family pool

Given the comparatively large sums required to invest in property it might make sense for a (close) family to pool resources for greater tax efficiency and to spread risk. Property investments could then be 'broken up' into tax-efficient chunks (as with unit trusts or directly held shares) so that each family member used his/her annual CGT exemptions if properties were sold at a profit. Such arrangements would not suit all families. Weigh carefully the sacrifice of some personal flexibility and the risk of a family row against greater tax efficiency.

You do not have to sell to capitalise on your gain

You can effectively capitalise on your gain without selling and thus defer tax if you get your property revalued and refinanced so as to replace your initial capital with increased loans. Say you originally raised £750,000 against your own £250,000 to buy £1 million's worth of property. After five years, it is revalued at £1.3 million, and your lender agrees to refinance it on a continued basis of 75 per cent LTV (loan-to-value ratio). Your loan would be increased from the original £750,000 to £975,00 (75 per cent of £1.3 million). You could then re-invest the extra £225,000 as equity in a second property while still retaining a 25 per cent stake and all the rental income in the first to service an albeit increased loan.

[3] Practitioners series 1R150

Commercial property

Commercial property (if well-let) is less risky for the private investor

Commercial property, for example shops or small offices, let for unexpired terms of over ten years to professional occupiers such as partnerships and small industrial units represent secure income. If well located and let, it is arguably a less risky investment for private investors than residential property with shorter term lettings. Commercial property is also likely to be freehold, while residential is often leasehold. Private investors generally make up the majority of bidders at local commercial property auctions. Small lots tend to fall into one of two price ranges: from £100,000 to £1 million, or from £1 million to £5 million. Large lots, such as London's Carnaby Street, go by **tender** to institutional buyers and professional property players, or they are sold off the market to purchasers who can exchange contract and complete within strict time scales.

Unless you have a minimum of £250,000 to invest in commercial property, agents and advisers are less interested and you will have to do more of the work yourself. But with £250,000 you can use borrowings to buy up to £1 million worth of commercial property. Provided the purchase was reasonable and let to a good tenant, with say ten years plus unexpired on the lease, the mortgage would be relatively cheap, easy to raise, and with acceptable investment risk. Moreover commercial leases are normally on a Fully Repairing and Insurance (FRI) basis, so the tenant is responsible for all such costs. This is not so with residential investments.

Be highly selective, and buy only good quality commercial property in niche areas. Investment institutions such as pension funds, property investment and development companies along with owner-occupiers dominate the commercial property market. They employ specialists to analyse every inch of what they buy and sell. Blue chip office tenants insist on state-of-the-art premises. So it is not usually feasible for individual investors to buy major office blocks.

You are far better off investing only in commercial property that is already let, at least until you have gained the necessary experience to identify and raise the finance for a good unlet site. Funding an unlet property will be difficult and so it is best avoided unless it is part of a small portfolio of say three or four properties. Landlords of commercial property collect what could be described as a fixed income in rent, normally with a five-year upward-only review – meaning it is increased to market rental value on the review date. Any dispute over the increase would be subject to arbitration.

Buy commercial property, for future income, but limited capital growth

As stressed, commercial property is essentially an investment in a future income stream if let to a reliable tenant. Your lender can calculate precisely how much rent you will derive (at least until the next review or expiry of your lease). The lender assesses his risk by taking advice from a specialist valuer who considers the tenant covenant, quality of the property/location, comparables and open market rental value. You should get reasonable interest margins of 1–1.5 per cent over bank rate when borrowing to buy well-let commercial property. Rental growth, when achieved, converts to extra capital value.

Regional differences in value are skewed to areas of affluent population, commercial activity and good infrastructure. The UK's silicon valley and the major airports, sited in the south-east and M4 corridor, have underpinned property values there, but towns such as Leeds, Manchester and Bristol have also seen solid and improving growth in commercial property values/rental levels. A nice little shop, let to a national chain of newsagents or butchers in a busy high street in a market town in the late 90s yielded net income of at least 8–8.5 per cent.

Lloyds Bank's sales-and-leasebacks (on 15-year leases) in 1996 were seen as a golden opportunity for private investors. But evolving technology is changing high street retailing. Online shopping and banking will result in consolidation. The growth businesses of the future such as call centres, niche retailers, themed food outlets and shops for telecommunications/computer/financial services may well emerge as the most reliable tenants.

Well-let commercial property in the UK at the start of 1999 looked exceptionally good value when compared to 30-year government bonds (gilts) and cash. Bond yields were some 5 per cent and falling; cash on instant deposit still earned up to 6 per cent, long term interest rates were poised to fall under 5 per cent, commercial property yields were between 7 and 9 per cent depending on the unexpired term of the lease. The **positive yield gap** between commercial property and gilts (bonds) had widened substantially.

Property pros watch bond yields like hawks to see if they are getting a good enough risk premium over gilts. A high-yield gap suggests expectation of low capital growth and higher risk. In other words, in the low growth, low inflation outlook for the UK economy, commercial property will be viewed as a high-income investment rather than one for capital growth.

Property entrepreneur Martin Myers, who with Goldman Sachs owns £500 million worth of commercial property estate leased to the Department of Social Security argues:

'Forget inflation: it is an aberration, not the "norm". Some 98 per cent of all inflation since 1400 AD occurred between 1960 and 1990. With deregulation, the end of socialism and a global economy, we are returning to low inflation and a low growth economy. Prices will be driven down, not up. Income, not capital growth, is the new mantra.'

But property bulls are equally sure that low interest rates – notably in Euroland – will underwrite a strong bull run in UK property over the next few years.

Get independent professional advice on commercial property

Estate agents and auctioneers can only estimate what properties might fetch: but they are essentially shop assistants, keen to sell. Comparison of their guestimates with actual sale proceeds is the reality check. They should know about the current re-letting risk and the security of tenure but not what the property might be worth at the end of the tenant's lease. That is why you need professional advice on the structure and the lease before you can rationally decide whether or not to bid for commercial property at auction.

Penny-wise can be pound-foolish

Be prepared to pay a seventh to an eighth of a per cent of the property's value for an independent valuation, subject to a minimum £500–1,000. A desk-top valuation will cost less, and it can serve to line up indicative terms for a loan, so that you would not lose so much if you failed to secure the property. But if there are any doubts about valuation, it would be penny-wise and pound-foolish to save the price of in-depth appraisal that might value the site correctly. If the tenant is triple A and the unexpired lease long, you can relax with a desk-top valuation.

Avoid nasty surprises post purchase

After you have obtained a preliminary valuation from a surveyor and your solicitor has done a thorough search of the 'legals', you will be less likely to confront nasty surprises post purchase. For example, while in commercial property most leases provide for upward-only rent reviews, some leases also embrace downward adjustments – opening up great uncertainty about future income stream. Lenders are most reluctant to commit a long term loan on property with such leases. Another example: most commercial property leases state the tenant is liable for full repairing and insurance. But some specify F (internal) RI. In other words, you, the landlord, would be liable for any external repairs.

Beware 'over-rented' commercial property

Also ask a local surveyor's advice on how the rent currently earned on the property you want to buy compares with new lettings. You cannot value the desired property correctly unless you investigate the market thoroughly and can project realistically its prospects for rental growth at the next review date. If you buy an over-rented property – that is one that still benefits from an above-market rent which is a throwback perhaps to the time, say, in 1988/9 when rents peaked – you would pay a premium for it, but have no/low prospects of growth going forward. Over-paying for an ex-growth property is one of the greatest dangers for amateur investors.

Over-rented *can* work in your favour

In theory, you could be relaxed about buying over-rented property if the income more than covered the interest on your loan, and it was let to an exceptional covenant. You would use the (overpriced) rent both to service your loan and to pay down the debt so that even if you did take a hit on rent at the expiry of the lease, you would still be ahead, with a valuable asset and reduced loan-to-value liability. You could then afford to earn a lower rent because you would have a smaller loan to service, and also hold a bigger stake in the property. But you would sacrifice tax efficiency as the property would cost you more capital and produce extra taxable income. All the same, it might still be a profitable proposition.

Gearing is even more attractive in commercial property

Gearing commercial property is even easier than borrowing to buy residential sites because you can borrow against its rental yield. Commercial property loans are either fixed, or variable interest, but are gradually paid off in equal quarterly repayments (as rent is collected quarterly) over the term of the agreement. There can be interest only periods within the terms, when you would not need to repay any capital. Variable interest loans can be a gamble unless your rent gives you ample interest cover. But fixed-rate loans can be matched by the amount of rent you will collect and synchronised to rent reviews (usually every five years). However, fixed-rate loans lock you in when interest rates fall substantially or if you want to repay early. So consider carefully the term of a fixed-rate loan and synchronise it with when you are likely to want to sell your investment.

While a mortgage for a home loan is generally limited to four times your annual income, commercial property loans are backed by the property purchased. No other guarantee is usually required. Lenders will charge an arrangement fee of typically 0.25–0.5 per cent of the loan, but it can be as high as 1 per cent, subject to a minimum of some £500–1,000. Shop around and compare mortgage offers on a like-for-like basis.

Use a mortgage broker to avoid the pitfalls

Unless you know what questions to ask and/or your requirements are straightforward, use a top mortgage broker, not merely commission salesmen – although they will charge you between 0.3 and 1 per cent of the loan. That fee could save you thousands more in pernicious penalties for early repayment buried in the small print of typical loan agreements. Let the broker spot these pitfalls by negotiating with lenders on your behalf. On larger, more complicated deals, the services of a mortgage broker can substitute that of an accountant. The best mortgage brokers are technicians able to work out not just the loan amount to borrow but also the margin you should be paying over the cost of funds – which is the basis for the fix negotiated for your loan. They have the purchasing power to shave fractions off the lender's profit margin. They use the latest screen-based data to play with the numbers in short, medium and long term interest rates in order to forecast, fairly accurately, your costs, cash flow and the cost of breakage to you (and the profit to the lender) should you break the agreement and pay back the loan early.

The cheapest lender is not necessarily the best

Building societies can be sophisticated and knowledgeable about local property. If you know of one that fits that description then do negotiate your loan directly. There are bespoke loans available in commercial property lending so make sure yours is designed to suit your needs. Remember that in a long term loan agreement such as that for property investment, the cheapest lender is not necessarily the best. You want maximum flexibility which, should you need to draw on it later, could prove as good as money in the bank.

The four pitfalls to avoid when negotiating a commercial property loan are:

- Lack of clarity in terms and conditions of your loan facilities.
- Breakage cost: know the penalties of repaying early.
- Small print: understand the front-end costs and any exit fees.
- Complication: go for a straightforward loan agreement.

Early repayments and penalties

You might cash out of your property at a good profit, or find a better prospect and need to sell the first to finance the second, or you may need to re-finance your loan because circumstances have changed and it is no longer viable. In such cases, you may pay your loan back early.

But beware. Lenders normally charge a **breakage cost** if interest rates fall between the date of the commencement of a loan agreement and the date of early repayment. That is not all. They may also try to charge the interest margin (the percentage profit over the cost of money to them and what they charge you for it) as well as fixed-interest rate reduction when calculating breakage cost. They call that loss of profit. Moreover, while the lenders pass their loss of profit on to you, they are less keen to share with you **breakage profit** if interest rates go up, not down. If they take your early repayment of capital and re-invest it at higher rates, they make more profit, and so have their cake and eat it too.

You could go for a loan with an assurance company or a bank that offers 'substitution of security', which is agreement up front that rather than repay early, you would roll your original loan into another substitute property. That avoids breakage costs.

Note that in a dispute, the courts are more likely to enforce payment penalties by commercial borrowers than by home-owners. That is one of the reasons why building societies and banks do not usually fix rates for residential property loans for more than five years. The courts are inclined to protect home-owners and accept the argument that they did not fully understand the lender's claim to breakage costs and profits. But commercial property investors are supposed to be sophisticated and understand the costly implications of early breakage. So be sophisticated when raising a loan to buy commercial property.

The attractions of commercial property investment

- You can gear capital at reasonable cost to buy property let for ten years plus.
- The occupier (tenant) pays agreed rent to the landlord for the term of the lease.
- The rent is invariably subject to upward reviews, typically every 3–5 years.

- The tenant is usually responsible for full repairs, insurance and structure.
- Income should rise if the property is well located, of quality space and construction and let to good tenant/s.
- It is usually freehold (while residential property is often leasehold).
- It is not as labour intensive (while residential property can be).
- It is a less risky investment because it is easier to value/finance on the income it will generate.
- You receive rent in advance and pay interest in arrears.

But:

- The cost of entry is often high due to higher capital values and fees.
- The commercial property market is dominated by big professional players.
- Transaction costs are high: some 5.5 per cent to buy, and between 1 and 1.5 per cent to sell.
- The purchase and sale of property can be slow.

Checklist for buying commercial property

- Buy in a location with high sustainable tenant demand.
- Do not pioneer locations – but try to be among the first to buy improving sites.
- Get your financing right – gear your loan against the level of current income.
- Access the downside risks. Can the tenant go bust? Can you service the loan?
- Weigh up any physical constraints – you will pay for any flaws in a downturn.
- Take advice from a qualified surveyor on valuation and a solicitor on legals.
- Talk to local traders, check out rival local offices, shops and other amenities.

Residential property
Be a landlord in residential property

Direct investment in residential property is not just potentially profitable, for many private investors it can also be enjoyable to search for it, stake a good site, do it up and then let it. At various times, the returns are excellent. For example, you could have derived 8–10 per cent gross return on capital invested in a one bedroom flat in central London in 1998/9, when blue chip growth shares in the US, UK and Europe yielded less than 2 per cent, and long term bonds returned around 5 per cent.

Experienced investors in residential investment will tend to prefer unfurnished lets. The cost of replacement of furniture and redecoration can absorb a large part of your gross rental income. You can also let unfurnished residential property for longer – three years is not unusual.

The value of residential property is closely linked to changes in real disposable income. When interest rates and inflation fall, and/or wages rise, home-owners have more money to spend: mortgages are cheaper, so they tend to buy bigger or better homes. Tenants might pay higher rent when economic conditions are buoyant. But there is a point at which the mortgage option looks cheaper – and renting expensive. Keep your eye on that point: it is both a maximum target and a ceiling for the rent you could collect.

No longer essentially a play for capital gain

Traditionally, investment in residential property was geared to capital growth, not income. That was because for many years, under successive Labour governments, there was rent control. The relaxation of onerous anti-landlord legislation increased supply of rental accommodation, while demand also grew due to changes in social structure – more single-parent families, divorce, greater job mobility and inter-company transfer. This balance of supply/demand has boosted income prospects.

Over-supply of residential property-to-let increases the risks

Mortgage lenders in the late 90s recognised private investors were keen to buy-to-let property and started to offer landlords mortgage rates often more favourable than those for home-owners. A new breed of brokers was born, touting residential property as an investment package. While annual gross income was in double digits and you could borrow at 6.5 per cent a year, the favourable yield gap was compelling. Private investors piled into the market. But buy-to-let only if the rental income is sustainable and good enough to justify your costs, risk and hard work.

The main risk is over-supply so that some property will inevitably remain empty, especially if its location is not close enough to travel/shopping/leisure amenities. Low interest rates might also lead to a contraction in tenant demand as some people switch to buying rather than renting. That will cause rental income to fall, but may also underpin capital values as more buyers enter the market. Buy the property that fits your strategy, be it high income or high growth.

High occupancy is the key to good returns in buy-to-let residential property

The key to good returns from buy-to-let residential property is to achieve high occupancy rates. An empty property is an unrecoverable loss of rental income. Voids are inevitable and the cost of carrying the property empty for say two months a year should realistically be factored into your model. But you will avoid frequent voids if you buy property with likely tenants in mind. Research shows the majority of UK tenants are under thirty-five years old. About a quarter are in their first home; a like amount are relocating for work; the rest are either in-between rented properties, renting pending purchase, renting after marital break-up, or students.

It follows that the greatest demand is for accommodation with good shopping and transport links. One to two bedroom flats are the most popular rentals, but they must be immaculate and require little maintenance. Short term lets score higher rental income, but at higher risk of voids and greater cost of wear and tear. Council subsidised lets, for example, can earn as much as 25 per cent gross per annum and certainly well over 10 per cent. Company lets and housing associations can provide reliable and longer term rental income.

If you invest in the top end of residential property-to-let, you might earn premium rents, and/or derive high sale prices But it would cost more to buy and to finance, and it might possibly yield lower percentage returns. Exclusive property with unique features is riskier to buy and hold than property that appeals to the mainstream. Be wary of properties with swimming-pools/high-specification finishes that deteriorate when left vacant, even for relatively short periods.

It is often said of land that they are not making the stuff any more. But that does not make it less susceptible to the law of supply and demand. The timing of your entry into the field and the location of your property will determine its growth in rental income and capital value. A house that costs £100,000 to build might be worth £500,000 in Belgravia but only £150,000 in Brixton. It is not the value of the house that is variable, but its location.

Walk the streets

At the beginning, you must be prepared to put in as much time as you can spare viewing prospective purchases so that you build up detailed knowledge of a specific market before you invest. You have to research those areas where tenant demand can be sustained. In residential investment, you will derive greater capital growth from identifying areas that are becoming more gentrified. It is now perhaps a cliché to count the skips in any given area. But refurbishment and design to maximise use of space can drive capital growth, if you are prepared to put in more money and a great deal more work. Planning permission will also enhance capital value. Your back yard, given planning consent, could become a valuable property.

Remember: location, location, location

Be rigorous in your assessment of amenities within walking distance of your targeted property. It must be near public transport. Good dependable tenants tend to be employed young professionals or students who will not compromise their convenience. Generally speaking, student accommodation, particularly in university towns such as Oxford, Cambridge, Bristol and Manchester, is always in good demand and commands good rent. A residential property sited near a major hospital might be a good prospect for letting to doctors. Main city locations to which population with spending power is gravitating are generally reduced risk. Birmingham, Manchester and Leeds for example, were perceived as growth areas in 1999. In London, niche areas where developers have created branding, such as Brent Cross, Soho, Covent Garden and Notting Hill Gate sustaining tenant demand.

How to reduce your risk when buying-to-let residential property

- Buy in an area of sustainable tenant demand.
- Know your market – look at 30–40 comparable properties.
- Zoom in on a radius of about a mile for in-depth, pre-purchase research.
- Walk the streets: check out the amenities – from shops to tube stations or bus stops.
- Investigate any underground rumble noise or any other such flaw.
- Go to the pub and chat to locals: you might learn something useful.
- Look up at the Town Hall what recent redevelopments have been sanctioned.
- Find out what the planning policy of the area is.
- Line up your finance, surveyor and solicitor.
- When you think you have a good site, calculate the odds before you buy.

Estate agents

If you do not want to buy in auction, then contact, and cultivate, the two or three most active estate and letting agents in your patch. Make a point of identifying the estate agents that have an exclusive stock of properties. Spend time with the best agents: get to know them and draw them out on prices and conditions. Although in theory estate agents act for the seller, they want to shift property off their books quickly. If they get to know your needs, they should be quick to spot the property that will suit you and, hopefully, call you first. Independent agents can tell you, precisely, what prices were recently derived in sales and in lettings for comparable properties in the area of your choice.

However, if you are a new investor, you could be taken for a ride by estate agents' hype unless you are prepared to gain objective and detailed knowledge of a specific neighbourhood. Only then could you access and recognise value for money in a good site. Let the agents know you mean business; that you know your market, and can move quickly once they show you the right property.

Stop and plan your finances carefully first

During times of low interest rates, when you have easier access to cheap money, the temptation is to go for it. Don't. Plan your finances first.

- Start with a realistic target of rental of 10 per cent gross per annum on a des-res – could you earn that rent on the property under consideration?
- Compare the property and its potential yield with what else is on the market – would you do better buying another property at that price?
- Discount your calculations for contingencies such as repairs/downturn.
- If it all still makes financial sense, put down the deposit and complete. If not, remember the golden rule on timing. You might be in a sellers' market.

Financing residential property-to-let

Investment in any property allows you to gear a relatively small capital base through borrowings in order to buy an asset worth several times more and with potential for future growth. Some investors like to gear to the maximum when investing in residential property, and will borrow as much as they can, in some cases, and during some periods of boom, that can be 100 per cent.

While lenders will give you 75–80 per cent, or even more with insurance, of the value of your property, prudent punters may want to put down a 30–50 per cent deposit and borrow the rest, either via a **repayment mortgage** or an **interest-only mortgage**. With low inflation, there is no advantage in dragging out the payback of your property loan. If possible, opt for payback of 50 per cent of the loan within, say, ten years.

The lender will take future rental income from your property into account when calculating how much you can borrow. Your existing pay and borrowings may also come into that calculation, as with a conventional home loan. But, increasingly, lenders are differentiating loans for investment in residential property to let from home loans, and, for the former, they are lending on rental income. But you might get better terms for a loan if you released equity from your home towards a larger deposit on a buy-to-let property.

Whether you raise a loan via a repayment mortgage or an interest-only mortgage, depends on your circumstances. If you have limited capital but are bullish on the property market and can afford monthly finance costs, go for an interest-only loan. Fixed-rate mortgages of up to ten years are popular with landlords and lenders who want to budget with certainty. You may need life insurance to match your loan so that the debt could be paid in the event of your untimely death. Term insurance running for the ten years, or however long your mortgage runs, provides cheapest cover.

Shopping for finance

Shop around for a loan to invest in residential property. Talk to at least three lenders, and note down what each offers you. Then play one off against the other and agree to the terms that give you maximum flexibility. Confront such issues as redemption penalties, valuation fees, the mortgage indemnity insurance and the possible imposition of tied products, such as their buildings and/or contents insurance into the overall deal. You must tell your lender that you plan to let the property or you could be in breach of your mortgage.

Do not take more risk for small economies

Do not be tempted to assume more risk to score small economies when purchasing property. For example, unless your lender insists otherwise, you could, in theory, dispense with the services of a surveyor and make your own inquiries. But that would be cavalier. Shop around for a surveyor with reasonable charges and a sound reputation – approved by your lender.

Letting agents

You could also dispense with the services of a letting agent if you live within easy reach of your property and are prepared to give up your own time whenever necessary. These estate agents charge, typically, 10 per cent of full agreed rental term (plus VAT) for introducing a tenant and 12–17 per cent (plus VAT) for rent collection and managing any problems on your behalf. You decide which degree of service you want them to provide. They normally have a minimum letting charge and usually collect their fees in advance. You can negotiate over fees. Set charges were abolished years ago.

But dispensing with letting agents is not a practical option for most investors. They give you instant access to a large pool of prospective tenants and can reach, via relocation agents, companies seeking rental accommodation for their executives. Relocation agents do not normally talk to landlords directly. To avoid frequent voids and personal contact with tenants, use letting agents.

Managing agents

A managing agent is appointed by the freeholders of the property to act on their behalf in matters concerning management of the whole block – for example, the redecoration of the hall, installation of a lift or annual service charges. Freeholders cannot dispense with this type of managing agent.

Get your residential property right at the outset

Before you let your residential property, you should address every potential problem concerning its working order and decoration. Get it right at the outset and you will save yourself time and money later. You do not want to have to pay for major refurbishment every three to four years. It is more cost-effective to spend at the beginning and write it off against your first year's income. If you have the place decorated and working to the highest standard specifications, you will reduce the risk of voids and trouble.

High standards in the fixtures and fittings and good working order will attract and retain the best tenants at the best market rents. If you cannot do-it-yourself to a professional standard (some will argue that the standards of the so-called 'pros' in the market are not nearly high enough) you must at least know enough about redecoration, plumbing, wiring, tiling and carpentry to be able to project manage any jobs you contract out.

If you do not know what you are doing in the area of maintenance, redecoration or refurbishment, you may be 'rolled over' by builders, electricians, plumbers and decorators. You should be able to inspect the work while it is being done, and check that it has been done correctly, otherwise you are open to endless aggravation as problems surface later. As with any purchase, just throwing money at specific plumbing or rewiring problems will not ensure they are resolved to a high standard and cost-efficiency.

Rent accounting

Account for your rental business formally and precisely to ensure you get the tax breaks without tears. The entries should be listed in the following order:

- Income.
- Expenses (itemised) with supporting receipts.
- Sub-total of expenses.
- Net profit.
- Wear and tear allowance (10 per cent gross income less water rates/council tax which are normally paid by the tenant) if your property is let furnished.
- Taxable profit.

The precise ownership of the property must also be noted. If it is jointly owned, as described above (not to be confused with a partnership which is taxed differently), the tax liability will fall to each according to his/her share in the property and in the income.

You should note that the following running expenses are tax deductible:

- Finance charges.
- Council tax/ground rent.
- Insurance.
- Repairs/ maintenance.

- Water rates.
- Professional fees – agents/solicitors/surveyors/valuers/brokers.
- Service charges.
- Advertising/miscellaneous costs.

In the event of a furnished letting, if you opt to take a 10 per cent wear and tear allowance, you cannot deduct any allowance for replacement of equipment and furnishings as a general outgoing. Be reasonable and honest and use your common sense when applying the rules set out in the Inland Revenue's guide, and you should remain within legal limits. And you must file the following for tax purposes:

- Receipts for all expenditure, even incidentals like paint brushes.
- Accurate records of all income.
- Mortgage statements.
- All receipts for capital expenditure for capital gains purposes.

Refurbishing residential property

Property in need of refurbishment or with structural problems will often sell at a discount. If you buy it, repair or renovate it, and then sell it, you might score a good capital gain. But do not undertake such projects without due consideration of the cost, time and hassle involved. Even if you are capable of adding value to a run-down property, you must learn how to deal with planning officers, architects, builders and others. Otherwise buy properties that need only superficial redecoration and minor repairs.

The attractions of residential property investment

- When let to a reliable tenant, you get a regular stream of income, usually representing a good return on capital employed.
- You stand to make a good capital gain when you sell (if you bought right) after several years. That is a bonus on top of the regular return on your capital whilst you let your residential property.
- The purchasing power of your savings, when invested in property that generates good income, is far more likely to track the real cost of living –

irrespective of whether you are invested in an inflationary or deflationary period.

- This can be an excellent alternative 'pension' for investors planning for income in retirement.
- Your 'property fund' can be passed down to your beneficiaries.
- Tax breaks allow you to use tax-subsidised finance to grow a large capital asset from a small capital base.

But:

- On a Richter scale of aggravation, you hit the high scores when your tenant breaks his contract.
- You may worry, and suffer potential cash flow problems during void periods.
- You must be prepared to actively manage your residential property investment. That means putting in more personal time and being more involved than you would be with other investments, notably with shares or even commercial property which is less labour intensive.
- Direct contact with tenants can be stressful and time consuming.
- Fees paid to specialised agents to let/manage your property will erode your annual return from rental.
- Cost of maintenance and repairs due to wear and tear can be open-ended.
- Danger of over-supply of accommodation heightens your risk of voids and therefore of irretrievable loss of income.

Step 5

Be an Owner: Buy Shares

How to identify the winners among growth businesses that will outpace the rest and create real wealth for you over several years

STEP 5
Be an Owner: Buy Shares

It is not *when* you buy, but *what* you buy that will earn breathtaking future profits from shares. But you must adhere to my wealth creation mantra: persistence, patience and staying power. These *will* produce profits – promise!

The extraordinary characteristics of world class super-growth shares, like those of 'superhuman' athletes, are easily identified, but are not often all found in one business. Seek out the rarities of exceptional quality. When you have found them, buy their shares alone. Be elitist; you cannot invest in everything that moves and you wouldn't want to. Narrow your focus to only the best, and forget the rest. Stay invested in super-growth shares for keeps.

You cannot at the time of investing calculate how much you will make over several years. But you can, and you must, avoid mistakes that cost capital and confidence. You cannot eliminate risk of loss when buying shares but in this risk-reduced strategy you will concentrate on what to buy and not sell, and what not to buy.

When you sell the wrong shares, you do more damage to your future wealth than if you buy the wrong ones (and hang on to the dogs). Even if you sell shares of exceptional quality at a profit now, you are likely to be a loser long term by doing so. You would disturb a position that will become much more valuable in the future and you would lose your stake in the profit of an outstanding business.

The Linford Christies of shares will outpace all the others in your portfolio, so that even if you hang on to relative laggards, or keep out-right losers, star shares will keep pulling away from the rest. In time, you will not even notice the also-rans in your portfolio. Say you put an equal amount into a dozen shares, and after about a year, three lost 35 per cent on average, five others gained an average 8 per cent and the remaining four doubled. Your capital will have grown by 28 per cent.

The three losers would represent some 12.5 per cent and the five average performers, 35 per cent. But your four winners would account for 52.5 per cent. You see how the power of super shares can eclipse all the other investments. It is a mathematical truth that while you can lose only 100 per cent of your capital, there is no limit to how much money you can make. But you must hang on to your winners through thick and thin and not be tempted to take profits, unless for a rational reason – to re-invest better (see Step 6). Greed or fear are emotions – not reasons.

Picking the winners

So how do you identify the winners? What should you look for? What are these extraordinary characteristics that turn certain ordinary shares into licences to print money year in and year out?

Nothing is certain in investment. But just as you would not bet on a cart-horse at Ascot, so you must look for top form and brilliant jockeys to find the winners among shares. You must also avoid potential losers. A 25–1 long shot does not often win at Ascot. Meanwhile bookies make a fortune collecting silly bets. If you manage not to lose money in shares, you are more likely to make it over time because you will have the staying power to be patient and to persevere.

It cannot be stressed enough that which shares you buy (and do not buy) and how long you hold on to them will determine your profit. This is not a mathematical or statistical share investment system. Its success lies in risk reduction by buying shares only in extraordinary businesses and holding them for many years, so that you gain the compounded effect of their growth and ride out stock market setbacks. Good investor behaviour and discipline are critical to success (see Step 7).

What not to buy

The following list is not comprehensive. No doubt money can be made from some, or possibly all, of the following but in this risk-reduced strategy, you would eliminate them from your investment universe.

Commodities, foreign exchange and derivatives

These markets often throw up price anomalies which specialists try to spot and bet against. They might make money but unless you have specialist skills, intuition and big money, you would be up against long odds. You are not in the business of speculation, but sound, long term investment.

Stock tips

Never try to make a quick profit out of shares. Only buy shares you are comfortable to hold long term. You are committing your money to a business that you do not manage yourself, so be business-like, do your own homework and rely on your own judgement before entering this 'partnership'.

Highly regulated businesses

Businesses such as utilities (although not high-flying telecoms) and tobacco stocks have proved profitable in certain periods but they carry inherent political risks to investors' wealth. Do you really want to bet on the whims of politicians?

Situations subject to pending litigation

If you own shares in a company against which the writs fly, weigh the risk/reward ratio of staying invested. Then make a sensible decision. Risk reduction rules out buying into such situations. Do you really want to bet against lawyers?

Businesses you are unable to understand, evaluate or monitor

High technology, biotechnology or other such futuristic businesses are subject to rapid change and so are not compatible with a buy-and-hold strategy. But if you are logged on to hi-tech innovation, ignore the above and press enter.

Shares in foreign economies, notably emerging markets

Invest in emerging economies indirectly, via shares in successful multi-nationals. Why bet on the macro-economics of Brazil, Russia or China when you can instead ride the likes of Coca-Cola, Gillette or Nestlé into these markets? Stay within the business environment you know, understand and can monitor easily.

Recovery situations

The promise of recovery is often in the price – thus increasing the risks from failure.

Unconventional instruments

Stay away from such securities as medium grade corporate bonds, options and warrants unless you can understand the risks. These instruments are for specialists. Do you really want to bet against the pros?

Special situations

They include potential takeover targets and companies under pressure to restructure. They are best left to specialists or confined to your (small) speculative fund (see Step 7).

Companies run by flamboyant/high-profile individuals

They may combine the role of executive chairman and chief executive. These 'driven' types are often not leaders but loners. They stifle initiative, stoke up resentment and chase away talent. Invest in disciplined, low key companies that never lose sight of their principal objectives: to satisfy customers, to motivate staff and to create value for shareholders.

Companies whose shares offer an inordinately high yield

There is usually something wrong. The high yield reflects the higher risk in buying and holding them. But growth companies with rising dividends are not taboo.

Companies priced at a premium due to expected radical restructuring

Forget it, particularly if those responsible for getting the business into a mess are still there, and stand to gain a 'performance bonus' if they clean it up. But when a new leader is appointed from outside, that often signals dynamic change and should be viewed positively.

Companies with limited outlets

Small cap stocks, unquoted shares or those quoted on junior markets. You could make money from shares in fledgling enterprises. But unless you are (legally!) on an inside track, leave them to those better able to access the risks and rewards. Punitive bid premiums or 'spreads' and lack of liquidity in small cap stocks is also off-putting. Size itself, whether small or large, is not the criterion when buying shares. But you want stakes in quality businesses with predictable future growth – which usually rules out small cap stocks.

Cyclical companies

By definition, businesses whose fortunes ebb and flow with the economy are not compatible with a 'perpetual' long term investment strategy.

Investment in shares is an art not a science. Dogmatic rules on what not to buy, such as those listed above, can be challenged but they *will* reduce risk. If you are confident you can make money breaking these rules, go ahead but like great art, investment involves diligence, discipline and skill. The taboos listed above require specialist knowledge.

Others to avoid

You should also avoid the following for fundamental reasons.

Industries where there is over-capacity

Favourable balance in supply/demand is what you want. It leads to higher sales and earnings. But over-capacity (too much supply in relation to demand) curbs sales growth, endangers profit margins and invites entry of new 'cut price' competition. Damaging price wars may result.

Industries with slowing growth in demand

It is not over-capacity (supply), but lack of demand that is the problem here. Falling sales and profit margins are the symptoms; slower future growth the likely outcome.

Businesses with strong market positions, but near the point of saturation

Likely to deteriorate in the medium term unless they move into growth areas that compensate for slower growth in their traditional market.

Companies with excessive debt

Even if management swears it can be comfortably serviced from existing cash flow. Debt burden puts future profits in danger from higher interest rates and/or a slow down in sales – factors that the management cannot control.

Labour intensive businesses

Exceptional growth companies can transcend the above taboo.

Capital intensive industries

Ship builders, property developers and the like do not normally achieve a high return on capital employed.

Industries with ease-of-entry

The number of participants increases and competition intensifies.

Cheaper priced companies with second rate management

They are usually cheap because of their inferior quality. Growth is stumped through bureaucracy, poor cost/risk control and lack of leadership. If the business has a decent franchise, you might buy the shares for the wrong reasons, i.e. it might attract a takeover bid. But confine such punts to your speculative fund (see Step 7).

It may seem as though there is not much left, and it is true that only a few outstanding businesses fit my criteria. But if you want to see real growth, you must stick to the outstanding ones.

Here are six **DO** rules on how to construct and maintain a growth share portfolio.

1. DO keep it simple
Your investment goal is to consistently derive above-average total returns – that is growth in dividends and share price – over many years. So invest only in a few proven, well-managed companies with almost inevitable growth. 'Normal' average total return from the stock market is 10 per cent per annum. Above-average companies should beat that.

Even an average 10 per cent total return will produce 2.59 times growth in ten years. An average compound rate of 12 per cent will triple your money in the same time. So keep it simple and pitch your expectations to a realistic average of between 10 and 12 per cent a year over five, ten or more years.

2. DO decide how much you can invest in shares over many years
You must have staying power, so plan to buy-and-hold shares through thick and thin. How much you invest in shares depends on your goal, age, risk tolerance and time horizon (see Step 2). Some 75 to 80 per cent of your free funds is probably about right over ten years plus. Around 60 per cent over five years represents only moderate risk – as long as you pick the right stocks.

3. DO narrow your focus to businesses with:
- Strong global consumer franchises with world brands and reputations.
- Large, liquid capitalisations: companies whose shares are easily marketable.
- Dominance: they are respected and emulated in their particular industries.
- Ability to grow sales, market share and profit margin well into the future.
- Products/services that command customer/staff respect and loyalty.
- Solid balance sheets: check in annual reports issued by the company.
- Visible earnings, strong cash flow: look for high return on capital employed.

- Clear strategy of long term growth, not just financial manipulation of assets.
- Coherent actions, not just words, to demonstrate strategy and leadership.
- Fiercely competitive management that is determined to be successful.
- Ingenuity, so that the business is constantly re-invented for future growth.
- Ability to pre-empt and respond to changes in consumer trends/markets.
- Management that is uncompromising in its pursuit of quality/profit.

4. DO stay focused on the long term prospects for specific businesses

Imagine you are Mr or Ms Big, buying shares in a private business. You, not the stock market, must determine what are its attractions, prospects and potential risks.

5. DO ignore the daily deluge of data that affects share price movements

It represents a reaction to, and reflection of, the here and now. It serves traders and speculators rather than long term investors. But note, and if necessary act upon, factors that are detrimental to the long term outlook for any of your shares (see Step 6).

6. DO compound your profit

Plough cash dividends back into your shares through direct re-investment programmes. You authorise the company to use your cash dividends to buy additional shares for you. You can opt out of the programme whenever you choose. But if you can afford to forgo income now, stay locked in. You will accumulate more shares and compound your total returns at no, or low, additional cost.

Perhaps even more importantly here are six **DON'TS** to remember when directly investing in shares.

1. DON'T attempt market timing

Trying to buy cheap and sell dear, or vice versa, is fraught with difficulty and it does not work. It is far better to buy-and-hold good shares. Let me tell you about Albert Einstein. When he went to heaven he found, to his great irritation, that he had to share lodgings with three others. 'What is your IQ?' he asked the first.

'It's 140, Mr Einstein,' the other replied.

'Good, good, we can discuss my theory of relativity,' said Albert. 'What about yours?' he enquired of the second.

'Its only 120, Mr Einstein,' he was told.

'Ok, fine, we'll talk about new movies.'

Finally, he repeated his question to the third, who replied:

'Its only 80 Mr Einstein.'

'So where is the stock market going?' asked the learned gentlemen.

So this could be Einstein's other theory: Only schmucks try to forecast the market.

2. DON'T worry about not doing conventional research

Number crunching and the study of complex comparisons and detailed sector analysis is for professionals – who often do worse than amateurs when picking which shares to buy. Rely on common sense, personal experience and good judgement.

3. DON'T sell – see Step 6 for the only valid (economic) reasons

Unless you have made a glaring mistake, identified a better opportunity or there has been an adverse change in the long term fundamental prospects of any given business, why sell its shares and disturb a position that will be more profitable in the future?

4. DON'T be distracted by short term outlook

You cannot forecast stock market crashes, recessions, floods, hurricanes, earthquakes or wars. Nor can the pundits: they are only guessing. Use long term logic to pick shares in great, world-class businesses – wherever they happen to be.

5. DON'T deviate from this consistent, systematic approach

Although consistency can be an excuse for not thinking, in this case it will keep you out of harm's way. The psychological aspects of owning shares can be disturbing. In market declines – or indeed in booms – your emotional responses could lead you to doubt/change your strategy, and thus deflect you from your goals (see Step 7).

6. DON'T buy shares on margin

That means buying shares on borrowed money. Stockbrokers – particularly in the United States – are eager to entice you to buy shares in this way. You put up only an agreed percentage of the cost and the broker lends you the rest. The shares are held in a 'street name' that is not your own, so that the broker can sell if the price falls and you do not put up more cash. Volatile shares such as those in the Internet sector usually require higher margins. The lender/broker earns interest on your borrowings as well as commissions on the purchase/sale of shares in your account.

Simple arithmetic shows that shares bought on borrowed money will have to grow in value above the cost of the borrowings before you make any profit. In the meantime you will effectively hand over control of the timing of your investment decisions to the lender. You simply cannot afford to borrow short to invest long.

Pick sectors according to your own knowledge and experience

It is easier to start the process of picking the right shares if you first decide which sector/s you know and understand. This is when you must identify and confront your personal strengths and limitations. Be honest with yourself. You should adhere to the twelve principles listed above, but that is not all. You must take into account your interests, experience, competence and goals. In short, your share portfolio should reflect your situation in terms of finances, knowledge and lifestyle.

Identify businesses with all or most of the characteristics outlined here, and buy their shares. You will own stakes in a collection of companies of rare quality. During the 90s these might have included IBM, Coca-Cola, Gillette, Nestlé, L'Oreal, Nokia, AIG, AXA, Merrill Lynch, Charles Schwab, Pfizer, Merck, Procter & Gamble, Vodafone, Johnson & Johnson, SmithKline Beecham and Glaxo Wellcome. Perhaps not all, but most of these will keep on growing well into the new millennium.

World class businesses such as these tend to be highly defensive in an economic recession. They are also well positioned to grow above average during economic expansion. They tend to supply products or services consumers absolutely need or want, such as drugs, food, insurance, personal care products such as toothpaste, over-the-counter medicines, toilet paper and nappies. In affluent economies, consumers also want, and can afford, personal computers, mobile telephones and financial services.

Rapid changes in Russia, Eastern Europe, the Middle East and South East Asia since the 1980s, have brought emerging economies into the capitalist system. Global deregulation, low inflation and the low cost of capital will continue to favour dominant companies with worldwide reach. Moreover, new technology has transformed their cost structures and now they are lean, agile and highly capital efficient. They can defend their leading position, and capitalise on what they do better than smaller rivals.

The case for concentration in your share portfolio

You will make more money by directly investing in a few good shares than you would via a collective fund. You would also not have to pay management fees, except to yourself. Diversification – the spreading of risk over fifty or more shares via a collective fund – is neither the most lucrative investment strategy nor necessarily the safest. You might still lose capital in a badly managed, diversified fund. You would be most unlikely to make the outstanding profits possible from concentration on only a few of the finest quality shares. Reduce your risk by focusing your shares on three or four industries with opposite risks so that they foil each other.

Shares in growth businesses with world franchises represent low risk opportunities to make substantial profits. That is why my strategy concentrates money directly into shares of a few – say eight to twelve – of these outstanding businesses. I make no apologies for the relatively small number. The uncommon, exceptional and rare are few and far between. Besides, if one share out of a dozen went down, that would represent just over 8.3 per cent of your capital. If one out of eight failed it would wipe out 12.5 per cent of your fund. That is a tolerable risk for the compelling reward of gearing your portfolio for maximum profit.

Of course, the rules above can't absolutely guarantee you a risk-free portfolio, but they will help you to eliminate long shots and to identify the best prospects, so that you can buy and hold them with conviction.

Now start your research

First look for companies in dynamic sectors where positive change is taking place. Key questions are:

- Do you know and understand the critical driving factors in this industry?
- What has changed in this industry?
- What is going on now?
- Which companies are leading the changes?
- Which company is most likely to gain and/or retain leadership?

Before buying shares in specific companies, ask:

- Is the management outstanding?
- Does it have a clear vision of the field ahead, so that they can continue leading?
- Is the business highly concentrated on what they do best?
- Look at the track record, and current management. Can management maintain leadership?

When you buy into only world class businesses, you buy a ticket to ride faster economic growth in some parts of the world at a time when more mature markets may have slowed down. A brilliant multinational company has built-in diversification of risk in its wide geographic spread.

You do not want shares in global imperialists, but rather multinationals that are locally specific. They will nurture workforces that reflect the cultural diversity of their markets and customers. Diversity helps them to understand the complexities of world markets and to communicate with the different cultures that they serve.

The world's most admired companies

The all-stars in the world's most admired companies tend to be big and American. Look at *Fortune* Magazine's 1998 survey of The World's Most Admired Companies, or the *Financial Times'* version, entitled The World's Most Respected Companies. What will strike you first is that big American companies dominate all but four of the twenty-one sectors researched. Second, not a few of the American all-stars are veterans in the world marketplace, but appear to be growing like young adolescents.

These include General Electric, Coca-Cola, Walt Disney, Pfizer, Merck, Johnson & Johnson, Merrill Lynch, IBM and Boeing – all in the top 25 out of 278 companies in *Fortune*'s 1998 survey. In the top ten are Microsoft, Intel, Hewlett-Packard and Dell – leaders in technology and consumer electronics. Sony of Japan is also among them.

These leaders are likely to remain in front for many years yet, even if, while moving rapidly forward, they occasionally stumble. What they have in common is focus, global reach and cogent strategic vision.

The four sectors in *Fortune*'s survey not dominated by American enterprises are food (Nestlé), petroleum refining (Royal Dutch/Shell), airlines (KLM) and cars (Toyota Motors). Why is it that American companies have dominated world business for so long?

First, American executives are born into a highly entrepreneurial 'can-do' culture which richly rewards risk takers and does not stigmatise failure in business. On the contrary, entrepreneurs in America who have tried but failed are more likely to raise venture capital than those with no experience.

Strong fiscal and cultural support for entrepreneurs in America has spawned explosive creativity in global industries such as high technology, pharmaceuticals, film-making and financial services. America may not have a monopoly on innovation and enterprise but its corporate talent is nurtured by the state and US shareholders, who encourage risk takers. By contrast, institutional investors in the UK and Europe are less inclined to sacrifice profit now to sanction initiatives for future growth.

Second, American business has long since embraced and mastered computer technology. In Europe, businesses remain comparatively under-invested, and employees unskilled in IT.

Superior world class companies tend to have flat organisations with wafer-thin layers of management. The power to make rapid decisions based on local opportunities and circumstances lies with those at the sharp end, who are best placed to capitalise, like entrepreneurs would, on changes.

Management of superleague companies are not easily fazed. In the turmoil of the crisis in South East Asia in 1997/8, they had the confidence and guts to invest for the future. Witness the billion dollar purchases of businesses in beleaguered Asia by corporate investors such as GE Capital, General Motors and Merrill Lynch. In contrast, institutional investors sold Asian stocks to cut short term portfolio losses.

Corporate leaders seize new opportunities – before they become threats. They do not benchmark themselves against rivals. Their standards are higher than those of their peers. Their top executives are opportunistic and energised when faced with changes in their markets. They constantly challenge the status quo and seek ways to regenerate, and, if necessary, re-invent the business for strong future growth. This renewal process keeps the business innovative, strong and in pole position. Staff do not go to work for such companies to fail. Their performance is monitored, as much to reward the best as to weed out the worst.

Not all blue chips are good prospects. We can all think of at least a dozen Footsie-100 companies that consistently fail to excel. These are the *hoi polloi* of the corporate world, in the second and third divisions. Their failures, boardroom rows, diversifications and 'shock' results are the stuff of daily financial reporting. Laggards blame factors beyond their control, such as the weather or level of sterling for their poor performance. They are cart horses on the corporate race track.

Example – Fallen Angels

But when the bookies' favourite falls, the press and the stock market put the boot in. Take Marks & Spencer in 1998/9, when prices on the high street were falling. Its competitors imported £14 billion worth of cheap goods from the Far East, but M&S imported only £1.4 billion worth, and stuck stubbornly to its high margin strategy. Sir Richard Greenbury, former chairman and chief executive, declared: 'There is a blood bath out there.' The reality was that canny customers had crossed the road for better value.

A boardroom power struggle ensued, which Greenbury and his would-be successor Keith Oates, both lost. Profits all but halved and M&S shares were dumped. The board, then led by 'lifer' Peter Salsbury, was forced to rethink even sacred dogma, according to M&S – and consider instead raising cash from its properties, accepting major credit cards and sourcing at least 50 per cent of its goods overseas. The column inches of bad publicity in 1998 would have cost M&S £150 million in advertising.

About the same time, Shell fell. It had rigidly stuck to investing for long term growth while the oil price plunged to some $10 a barrel. Its rivals merged to cut their costs. At Shell, the wake-up call to restructure its sprawling empire came only after its profits plunged and it had to write off billions of dollars. It had failed to produce a decent return on capital employed, a tidy focused portfolio of assets, cost discipline, and earnings growth – legitimate demands of investors who own the business.

Both Shell and M&S were once leaders in their respective fields. But they got too stiff (arrogant) and too fat in the belly (overmanned and bureaucratic) to win any races in today's highly competitive global market. M&S has yet to grasp the nettle of building a global retail brand. It must also re-invent its UK business to defend its dominant but saturated market share in clothing. Consumers now spend more on PCs, mobile phones, DIY and financial services. At Shell, the shock has wrought a revolution in strategy and structure.

The 'fight or flight' response of these two fallen angels in the face of their respective difficulties will determine whether they still have the right stuff to come back. Their corporate genes are good. Their respective balance sheet strength is formidable. Strong businesses can survive limited periods of weak management. But protracted deterioration leads to irreparable damage.

Also, like star athletes, companies can become cocky, deteriorate and never fully recover their form, while others may falter but come back all the stronger. Coca-Cola, for example, made a disastrous mistake when it launched New Coke in the mid 80s. But it reversed its strategy and used the mistake to re-enforce consumers' loyalty to Coca-Cola Classic.

Example – Rising Stars

Like athletes, star companies are single-minded in pursuit of the top prizes. For example, pharmaceutical companies must plough substantial profits back into research and development in order to maintain a healthy pipeline of new products. They must also invest in marketing and sales to score profits now. The weakest drug companies in Europe and in the US merged in the 90s to gain critical mass and the funds to bolster their scientific and marketing power. A handful had it all – high scientific scores in R & D, promising new products in the pipeline and great marketing power. Among them, America's Pfizer, which narrowed its focus to discovery of new drugs throughout the early 90s – at the expense of its popularity on Wall Street.

At the beginning of the decade, Pfizer's portfolio of products ranged from perfume to pigments, chemicals and catheters. By 1999 Pfizer, led by Bill Steere, had sold off all the distractions to its core drugs discovery business. Its share price increased almost eight-fold in the five years to the end of 1998. Pfizer had it all.

It costs (in 1999) some $600 million to develop a new drug. A blockbuster can earn in excess of $1 billion a year for several years, until its patent runs out. But many other drugs do not even recoup their development costs. It is not just a question of throwing money at the scientists in the labs. Drug companies must access promising projects almost as astute venture capitalists might. While a high proportion of their R & D is planned, it is based on probability, not certainty.

Pfizer is of a calibre that can sustain risk of losses from expiry of patents or failure of drugs in the late stages of their discovery, and also capitalise hugely on opportunities. New discoveries can be serendipitous. For example, Viagra was discovered by accident, but Pfizer had the science, initiative and marketing clout to exploit it. High scientific scores bring in a bonanza of new drugs. Their sales pay for R & D and marketing. This virtuous circle is created by sacrificing some profit in the short term.

Keep your eye on the business

You must regularly – at least once a year, if not every six months – review your share portfolio. Re-examine rigorously the reasons why you bought the shares in your collection. Are those reasons still valid? Do not worry about falls in share prices due to general market decline, or anticipation of a bear market. But do watch out for deterioration in the business in which you own shares. If it has fallen behind its peer group, there may be a serious problem, and you might decide to sell. Never hold shares in a company losing market share. The risks in selling are discussed in Step 6.

The advice industry constantly stresses that directly owning shares, as opposed to units in a pooled fund, is riskier. Such advice is surely not predicated by the substantial fees earned from selling pooled funds to clients. It stems rather from the general misguided assumption, discussed above, that greater diversification equals less risk. But if you are disciplined and consistent in your choice of which *quality* shares to buy and when to sell them, you will have an advantage over the market and reduce your risk of loss.

The majority of other shareholders are professionals, or amateurs who invest their capital in pursuit of short term profit. A growing number of day traders – private investors who buy and sell shares online in a matter of weeks, days or minutes – means there are even more short-termists out there.

The professionals are under acute commercial pressure to perform in the short term. Day traders often deal on borrowed funds, so must cut and run, whether with a profit or a loss, but you can afford to take a long view of the prospects of the companies whose shares you own. That gives you greater resilience.

It is more risky to be out than in

There is high risk of capital loss if you have to sell shares in unfavourable market conditions. The markets oscillate between greed and fear but the biggest risk long term is to be out of the stock market. Shares are the best investment over time. No other form of easily accessible investment can generate real wealth both in terms of growth in capital and increased income (dividends).

Shares have been by far the most rewarding investment over the past eighty years. According to investment bankers CSFB, whose respected Equity Gilt Study compares historic returns on shares, cash and fixed-income investments in the UK, £100 invested in an equity fund in 1918 would have topped £1 million by the end of 1998, as long as all the income was re-invested gross.

That same £100 invested in gilts in 1918 would have grown to a mere £13,315 by 1998, and if left to decompose (through inflation) in a cash fund, it would be worth only £7,038. After adjusting for inflation, the £100 invested in shares would, in 1998, have bought a small house, but no more than a small second-hand car if invested in gilts, and a measly weekend away for two had it been stashed in cash.

Now 1998 happened to be a bumper year for investment returns in the UK. Conventional gilts were the best performing asset class and delivered 21.7 per cent real total return, while shares produced 10.6 per cent and cash 4.9 per cent. But investment in shares will produce more profit than from gilts and/or cash over the longer term, especially if your dividends are automatically re-invested gross into more of the same shares.

Indeed, the CSFB study shows that appreciation of the original capital invested in shares was only a very small part of the total return delivered to investors over eighty years. It was the re-investment of dividends gross that compounded the capital invested in shares, and resulted in almost 98 per cent of the total return produced.

Note that rising share prices and *not* the dividend income itself produced nearly all that spectacular performance so do not read CSFB's study as a recommendation for high-yielding equities. On the contrary, the findings show that £100 invested in the high-yielding engineering sector at the end of 1964 would have led to gross dividend receipts of £626, while for the lower-yielding pharmaceutical sector, gross dividend receipts would have totalled £5,556 over the same period to end 1998. In other words, so-called low-yielding growth shares produced around nine times more in dividends than shares in a high-yielding sector. Moreover, returns due to the capital appreciation of re-invested dividends for the pharmaceuticals sector were thirteen times greater than those for the engineering sector. You can see why growth businesses, which often command a premium in their share prices, are good value.

These figures are inflated because income would not normally be re-invested gross, as it is taxable. All the same, they still prove that shares are by far the best investment, even in periods when all types of assets increase in value. The almost fantastic profit from superior growth shares held for many years is not a hit-or-miss gamble.

Pundits who proffer prognostics of a future fall in the average real return on shares base their pessimism on the belief that 'it cannot continue'. But extraordinary global businesses can, and will, beat the average, whether quoted on the UK, US or European stock markets.

Some of your shares will not work out, but the winners will more than compensate. However, it is vital that you stay invested through bad and good years to smooth out the fluctuations and reach your long term target.

Inflation, especially if you are under forty, is still the enemy. Although it might appear subdued now, it could strike again in the future and erode the purchasing power of your money. Even if inflation remains at a relatively benign 2.5 per cent or less, you may have to make your capital and income stretch over a longer retirement, given better health prospects but a shorter working life.

Annuity rates are lousy when interest rates are low. When you retire, you may be eventually forced to buy an annuity with 75 per cent of your personal pension fund.[4] You could be locked into a low return for the rest of your life, and be unable to maintain your lifestyle and financial independence in middle to old age. That is a far bigger risk long term than volatility in share markets now.

Even if you are now in your fifties, fully employed with a defined benefit pension and among the nation's top wage earners, you cannot assume you will keep your job – and full pension rights – until 'normal' retirement age. Do not count on employers or the government to solve the problem of your underfunded pension: rely on yourself.

Alternative dividends

Dividends are important but they come in different forms. Do not zero in on cash dividends when deciding what shares to buy. Businesses that pay high dividends without strong growth in sales and profits are not healthy, and should be avoided – as noted earlier. In this strategy, you would buy shares only in dynamic growth companies. Do not expect them to pay out

---

[4] As rules currently stand you must buy an annuity by the time you are seventy-five but there is pressure on the government to change these rules.

every penny of their profit in dividends, rather they will plough profits back to secure future growth. You will receive gradually increased amounts of dividend over many years.

Companies willing to subjugate dividends now for greater future profits are the ones to back. When Pfizer in 1997 said its growth would be lower because of increased R&D, the market's initial reaction was to sell Pfizer's shares. Jam tomorrow is anathema to the market, but should not be to you and me.

Private investors will also find it tax efficient to buy-and-hold shares in growth companies. That is because capital gains can be deferred (by not selling) or reduced with careful tax planning. But cash dividends attract tax at the investor's highest rate.

Share buy-backs

Many companies have responded to a wider preference among investors for capital growth rather than high dividends with share buy-backs. During the 90s, top executives also received a large part of their remuneration in stock options. They had an affinity of interests with shareholders – everyone wanted their shares to go up. Hardly surprisingly, executives voted for share buy-backs.

Leading companies have bought back their shares and not issued new ones. Buy-backs normally drive share prices higher because cash surplus within the company pays a low return, but debt finance is tax-deductible and usually enhances earnings per share and reduces cost of capital. Share buy-backs also alter the balance of supply and demand of shares in the stock markets.

Sceptics argue that buy-backs have shrunk the supply of top shares, thus pushing up their share prices. But it is sensible that corporate finance departments within prosperous companies opt to return surplus cash to shareholders rather than hoard it. On the contrary, companies that borrow funds to buy back their own shares might be open to criticism. Managers should not take on risk, via more debt, to push up their shares.

Tracker funds

Buy-backs at large-capitalisation blue chip companies have had a further knock-on effect. Tracker funds (or **index funds**), which shadow the leading indices, have had to increase their weightings in large capitalisation stocks, and have chased their share prices ever higher.

Takeovers and mergers

Another factor has shrunk the supply of large cap, blue chip stocks, and thus pushed up their share prices: takeovers and mergers. Billion-dollar deals in the financial services, drugs, telecoms and Internet industries have reduced the number of companies within those sectors. The remaining players are even more dominant and their shares have acquired greater scarcity value.

Top shares toppy?

Remember the stock market is an auction market where shares are priced at whatever buyers will pay. So valuations, even at peaks, must not be the deciding factor when you buy shares – it should be the quality of the business and its prospects. Sure, the multi-fold-plus rise of US equities since 1982 will be interrupted some time, like it was in 1987, and briefly in 1998, and you can be sure that the shares of extraordinary companies will come down with the rest. As an old Wall Street adage puts it, 'When the whore house is raided, all the girls are taken.'

But lower valuations for outstanding businesses will in due course tempt investors to buy their shares – fundamentals eventually determine share prices. If the market, as represented by the financial community, has high hopes of shares in general, or an industry or particular business, the price of the shares will be high. If the reverse is true the shares will be 'cheap', reflecting low expectations.

There is also a correlation between the **price earnings (p/e) ratios** of some companies' shares and the public relations that influences markets' current appraisal. The pr of a company, good or bad, can distort its p/e ratio temporarily. But eventually the company's earnings will drive how the market corrects its share price.

Superior companies are rarely cheap. Do not wait to buy them at bargain prices. However if their shares fall in a general decline, or because they disappoint the market short term, buy them aggressively. Even if you already own them, buy more if you have more money to invest.

Cheap is not necessarily good value

You can never pay too much for superior quality, although sometimes you can pay too soon! A great business might reasonably command a large premium, just as a Picasso or Vermeer will attract buyers at ever increasing prices. Cheapness in the mind of a consumer indicates inferior quality and defectiveness, but in stock market terms cheapness is often wrongly associated with great investment opportunity. In fact, cheapness in stock market terms usually signals higher risk.

Forget about buying low and selling high – good things do not come cheap. Buy shares in good companies that you understand, and adhere to the criteria identified in my strategy. Do not quibble over price when you buy, or wait to buy on dips. You may end up kicking yourself if their prices just keep going up and you do not buy.

When to buy

Great fortunes have been made by investors with enough cash and the guts to move smartly into the market after a sharp correction when bargains were available. But those who bought quality stocks after the October 1987 crash, and held on to those shares over the next decade, will know it is essentially what you buy, not when you buy, that will make you a fortune in the stock market. If you had bought second rate shares after the 1987 crash, you will not have done so well.

Market timing is a futile exercise – so do not attempt it. Since some 75 per cent of all trading in the stock market is done by professionals, your decision about when to buy (or indeed when to sell) is matched by someone with the opposite view. You have a 50/50 chance of being right the first time – but the odds will be stacked against you getting two correct moves in succession. You have to be right twice. If you do not repurchase the shares sold at cheaper prices later, then you will have gained nothing but a short term profit. No-one is consistently right about market swings. When you are wrong you can do a lot a damage – essentially by being out of the market and thus missing out on the up-swings.

You will probably lose money if you consistently try to call market turns, take profits, and switch from one stock to another – all actions which are short term and which only benefit brokers. Leave all that to the 'active' professional managers. You do not have to be constantly doing something; you just have to be right in your choice of which stocks to buy. Do not expect to get every share right – even if you stick to the buy rules.

Yes, timing can enhance returns if you buy great shares after a sharp correction. But if you sit on your cash, waiting for such an opportunity, you will miss the up-swings in a rising market. A stash of cash held to buy shares after a crash is fine in theory, but in practice few investors have the guts to buy when the majority is selling. When the market is falling, fear is in the air, and that will affect your confidence (see Step 7).

Devalued cash at the top of the market

Cash at the top of the market is not worth as much as cash at the bottom. When you take your money out of shares at the top you will effectively have devalued currency with which to buy other shares. Conversely, money that comes into the market at the lows has great purchasing power. But that implies you have taken a loss cashing out at low prices, or you have sat on cash.

You are far better off getting into the market and staying in for the round trip of ups and downs. You could keep a small fund of cash ready to top up core purchases whenever the market declines. But do not bet on your psychological ability actually to do so.

Cost averaging

The advantage of cost averaging is that it takes the guesswork out of when to buy and you don't need a large amount to get started. You put into place an automatic buy order for the same fund or chosen shares at a regular date and invest the same amount of money until you have bought all you plan to. This way you buy more shares or units when prices are low, and less when prices have moved up.

Over a year, your cost should smooth out wild gyrations in share prices if the market is going through turbulence. Depending on your psychology, you will be elated or deflated when you can buy more shares because they have gone down. Most investors instinctively like to buy shares after they have gone up, which is just as irrational as selling shares because they have gone down.

That is what day traders do when they watch their screens and buy the blue numbers (share prices that have gone up) and sell the red ones (share prices that have gone down). Both strategies might work in the short term but only fundamentals, not momentum, will determine share prices in the long term.

What John Maynard Keynes knew

Keynes recognised he was powerless against systemic risk and that market timing is a futile exercise. He wrote in 1938 that he had abandoned his once-held belief that profit could be made by what he called a 'credit cycle policy', namely holding ordinary shares in slumps and disposing of them in booms. He explained that increased market volatility meant that he had not been able to take much advantage of a general systemic movement out of, and into, ordinary shares as a whole at different phases of the cycle.

He said that in the early 1930s there had been two occasions when funds he managed depreciated by 20 to 25 per cent within a few months and he had not been able to escape the movement, even though on both occasions he had foreseen correctly what was ahead. Even so, he noted, his investment results were successful over the long term.

He concluded that wholesale shifts in investment strategy are impracticable and undesirable. He wrote: 'Most of those who attempt market timing either sell too late and buy too late, and too often do both, incurring heavy expenses and developing a too unsettled and speculative state of mind.'

Tips for good share ownership
Purchase shares in your name

Purchase shares in your own name, as opposed to a nominee account held for you by your stockbroker, and you will receive specific company news and results, along with dividends directly from the companies in which you are invested. It will also enable you to sign up for a direct re-investment plan.

Invest in collective funds for convenience and some tax efficiency

If you are a higher rate tax payer, there is some tax efficiency in investing in shares via collective investments such as pension funds, unit trusts and investment trusts. Collective fund managers can switch investments free of capital gains tax within the fund, while you cannot do this with directly held shares. However the UK dividend income of pension funds has effectively been reduced by 20 per cent by the cancellation of previous rights to reclaim payment of tax credits; and management fees must also be weighed up against any tax efficiency.

Use your capital gains tax exemption to reduce tax

Use your annual exemption from CGT (£7,100 a year in 1999/2000) to reduce tax on your capital profit. If you invest in unit trusts and investment trusts you will pay capital gains tax (or crystallise a capital loss) only when you sell your units or shares. The exemption effectively turns a capital gain from the sale of shares or units in a pooled fund into a tax-free income distribution. A married couple could, in theory, harvest more than £14,000 a year tax-free from successful investments in unit trusts, investment trusts or directly held shares.

Be passionate

Elitist investors have insatiable curiosity and a passion for ferreting out new consumer trends and new products and services. They don't just read financial papers and annual reports: they have broad interests and bring all that into their investments. Buying growth shares is a grown up form of shopping. As a wise old investor once told me, 'Investment, my dear, is like sex: enthusiastic amateurs do it better.'

Do not be resentful

Do not be influenced by snide press comment, or resent the high pay and generous stock options awarded to the people who run the companies you own. As long as they are outstanding, they are cheap at the price. For all the millions they take home, they usually live for the business and add value which far exceeds what they derive from it. Be pleased that exceptional people are working for you. If they hold a substantial part of their net worth in your company's shares, be delighted. As Warren Buffett has said, it shows they like to eat at their own restaurant.

Be clear on how much you should put into shares

Professor Jeremy J. Siegel of Wharton Business School in his book,

Stocks for the Long Run, logs market performance since 1802. The book includes numerous charts and graphs that provide a clear perspective, based on academic study, on returns and market fluctuations over a long period of time. This lacks some scientific accuracy, but it debunks the commonly-held view that shares are high risk, while bonds are not. Over time the reverse has proved true.

HOLDING PERIOD (YEARS)	1 YEAR	10 YEARS	30 YEARS
Minimum Risk	6.2	40	72.1
Conservative	25.0	62.3	91.8
Moderate	50.0	87.9	115.5
Risk-taking	75.0	106.9	134.6

RISK TOLERANCE (%)

The percentages advocated in Professor Siegel's table (above) are too aggressive within the context of my risk-averse philosophy. I should reject the suggested level of 106.9 per cent for a 'risk-taking' investor over a ten-year view. Any level of long term investment that assumes short term borrowing is in my view imprudent and would put you at the beck and call of the borrower. Even at these relatively modest levels of borrowing, you may be compromised in your freedom of action – if only psychologically.

Few investors can envisage a thirty-year horizon. But young investors should invest aggressively in shares – within the limits of what they can afford. Older investors who can afford to forgo income now and tuck away money for ten years should adhere to my guideline of putting 75 to 80 per cent into shares.

To summarise

Once you have decided how much to lock away directly in shares, stick to your plan. Stop talking to stockbrokers and fund managers in order to avoid short term decisions based on knee-jerk reactions. Stay within the parameters and criteria in this strategy. Choose your shares carefully and buy-and-hold them for many years. Discipline ensures that greed and fear are resisted, no matter how strong the temptations. You should not sell in a crisis, nor even when war is declared. On the contrary – buy from frightened people, unless you happen to be one yourself!

You can, and you will, do better at share investment than the professionals because you are likely to be more imaginative, less shackled by committee-think and more in touch with the real world. You are also dealing in reality – your own hard earned capital. You can bring your own subjective experience and perceptions into play to make investment in shares exciting and rewarding. You need not be a genius at mathematics but you should get out and about. Be curious about new trends in consumer products and services.

Example – Gucci

I know about luxury goods. I bought Gucci shares at $68 in 1997, and was pleased when they promptly rose to $75. I then contemplated buying more but in the end I didn't. In the event the Asian crisis in late 1997 decimated Gucci's shares. I was unable to buy more at half the price – it felt like throwing good money after bad. Nor did I sell as I stuck to my rules of when to sell and when not to. It was too soon to write this business off.

Gucci's shares fell to a low of $28. Still I could not justify selling on fundamentals. Gucci was a well-managed growth company with a global brand in quality products that satisfy universally shared aspirations to attain style, luxury and status. Such aspirations are human and do not go out of fashion, even though the deeply aspirational peoples of South East Asia had temporarily stopped power shopping. Gucci's management had also re-positioned the business for greater growth in Europe to balance out Asia.

There was a dislocation between what was happening in the stock market to Gucci's shares and what was my own experience in Gucci's stores and in the streets. Stylish women in the cities of the world sported $500-plus Gucci handbags, and Gucci loafers, loved by the European jetset, were hotfooting it over the world. I saw this, and in my column in the *Times* in early January 1998, I recommended buying Gucci's shares at $49.

Days later, France's LVMH, a major luxury goods group led by Bernard Arnault, revealed it had bought the 9.5 per cent stake from Gucci's rivals Prada. LVMH went on accumulating Gucci. Overnight, the market perception of the Italian fashion house changed, and it soared over the next few weeks to over $80, as traders bet on a bid. The fundamentals that prompted my purchase had not changed. With or without a bid, Gucci had scarcity value and the hallmark of an extra-ordinary growth business. It was one to bag and to hold.

Step 6

When to Sell – and When Not to Sell

The premature sale of winners is the most costly investment mistake – worse than holding on to losses. Do not sacrifice large future profits for small short term gain now

STEP 6

When to Sell – and When Not to Sell

Why sell?

There are four valid financial reasons to sell your shares. There may be many equally valid personal motives, such as to finance a family business, to buy a new home, to pay for your children's education or to make a divorce settlement, but such personal reasons are for you to consider and decide upon. My sell rules will help you meet your financial objectives when buying shares according to the investment strategy described in this book. That goal is to create real wealth from buying and holding shares in outstanding businesses over many years.

You must avoid a short term approach if you are to be successful in attaining this long term goal. Do not lose sight of what you want to achieve. It is easy to get confused and carried away by the highly contagious, manic, panic mood swings of the stock market when shares rise or fall precipitously. But you are *not* attempting to beat the market in day-to-day, week-by-week or month-by-month transactions. Nor do you have to be hyperactive in managing your share portfolio. You just have to be right more often than you are wrong about which shares to buy, and which to sell, after rational consideration.

The reasons to sell are:

1. You made a mistake. You bought shares in a business that is not of high enough quality to have and to hold over the long term.

2. You bought shares in a business that has since deteriorated, either because of a terminal decline in its market or it is losing market share because of bad management.

3. You have identified a better opportunity, but must sell something else to raise the cash to invest in it. You must be certain that the opportunity is definitely better before you take action.

4. You want to boost your annual income by harvesting some or all of your CGT-exempted allowance: wealth without extra freedom and comfort is not much fun.

Note the rules do not include selling shares that have reached your 'price target'. Shares in exceptional businesses do not necessarily come cheap, and may even from time to time seem overvalued. But their quality and sustained ability to go on growing earnings and dividends are rare qualities. This scarcity value is hard to quantify. So do not be tempted to take profits when your winning shares seem too high. You would cut growth out of your portfolio and damage your future wealth, unless you bought back the same shares at lower prices – and you would be lucky to do that.

Nor should you ever sell winners to buy shares that have underperformed in the same sector. You would risk doing double the damage to your wealth. Yet experts, on short term logic, often advocate inter-sector switching. This entails selling the stars that have outshone all the rest in the sector because they are 'too expensive', and buying shares that have performed less well because they are 'better value'. This is a risky strategy for a long term investor and one that is best avoided. Stay with quality. Ignore any price reactions as a result of others switching from your 'high priced' shares to 'better value' ones.

The risk in getting your sales wrong is increased by capital gains tax. If you have made a mistake and can use tax losses from selling it, then do not hesitate to do so. The profits from your winning shares will look less tantalising if you stop and work out your tax liability and after tax gain before you are tempted to sell them. Do not sell your winners. Rather, you should hold on to them even if you must ride a roller-coaster of volatility in the price. As stressed in Step 5, market timing is futile, so do not attempt it – you will be a loser in the long run.

If you accept that it is not *when* you buy but *what* you buy that matters, then you will also agree it is irrational to sell exceptional shares just because they 'have gone up so much'. Also that it is wrong to sell good shares because the market generally seems unsustainably high.

After working through the advice in Step 5 you will have been highly selective in your choice of which shares to buy-and-hold, and you will have made a commitment to stay invested through thick and thin. Now you are a partner in a thriving business that can materially enhance your future wealth, why would you want to sell out? Rather, stay invested in something good.

But that is not to say sleep on your shares. Remain constantly vigilant, and review rigorously every six months or a year the progress and prospects of the companies whose shares you own. Are the reasons that prompted your purchase still valid? What has changed? If you identify a valid reason to sell, act immediately, even if you must pay tax or take a tax loss.

So having established that there are four valid financial reasons to sell, we'll take a look at them in more detail.

A mistake

We all make investment mistakes. It is not always easy to distinguish long term growth companies from ones that are buoyed by short term market perceptions which soon turn out to be misconceptions. Or you may have been tempted to buy shares that appeared 'so cheap'. Now that they have become even cheaper, you realise they were not a 'value play', but just played out.

Denial compounds your investment error

Investment errors, based on mistaken identity or bad judgement, are easy to recognise but hard to admit. The joke about the investor telling his stockbroker, 'Sell when you see my buying price', reflects investors' natural reticence to admit error, and to take even a small capital loss. Most of us prefer to hang on to a loss on paper in the hope of at least breaking even before selling. But if you do not cut your loss on an inferior investment, you risk far greater future losses. Denial will compound your investment errors, so limit the damage by admitting them.

The same applies to property. When the housing market is depressed, the same emotions are prevalent. Activity is paralysed by homeowners' refusal to drop their asking prices. They do not want to sell for less than they paid which is understandable, but irrational if they want to re-invest in another property. They should cash out to take advantage of depressed buying prices. With property, as with shares, you must accept the prevailing market price if you *have* to sell. That is reality. Hanging on for a better price is self-indulgence that could cost you dear.

When you hang on to the wrong shares, you tie up your money in a bad investment and miss two opportunities. First, you would not be able to re-invest in another business that could produce substantial gains and more than make up for your losses. Second, you do not use tax losses to offset your gains. It is *salutary* to admit a mistake, take a loss and move on. Run your profits over many years but cut your losses quickly and you should achieve excellent investment returns.

Do not let your ego and emotions get in the way of sensible investment strategy. Even if you recognise a mistake quickly, you may be reluctant to rectify it immediately, or at all. Fight that reluctance – get tough with yourself. There is no shame in making investment mistakes. Admit yours, and act decisively to preserve your confidence and sense of purpose. It is not the mistake, but the management of it that will weigh on your finances in the long term. Note that a mistake, if you learn from it, is a valuable lesson. Recurring investment mistakes will result in repeated absolute loss, and must be avoided (see Step 7).

Self-punishment and pride are self-destructive

You will recover your capital and confidence much faster if you act decisively to reverse mistakes. It is easy to feel demoralised after a loss in your capital but to punish yourself by agonising over the loss in your capital is self-destructive. Instead, you should sell your losers and immediately re-invest the funds, even if you just buy more shares in your best-performing companies.

Your goal is to invest only in shares of successful businesses, and to let your capital grow several-fold over many years. You will thus compound the growth of your capital. Remember, you can lose 'only' 100 per cent on a bad investment, but you can make much more than that on a good one. So unless you sell a bad investment and re-invest in a good one, you will lose both the opportunity to recover losses, and to make a lot more money. So swallow your pride. Sell and re-invest to reverse your mistake.

Deterioration

You have concentrated your investment only into shares of élite companies with superior growth prospects. By so doing, you should have increased potential future returns and reduced risk of loss. Accordingly, the second financial reason to sell a share is when there is evidence of deterioration and likely decline in the long term prospects of the underlying business. It no longer fits the criteria that prompted you to buy its shares.

It is important to identify deterioration before everyone else, or you will miss the opportunity to sell at a good price. When the market is over-sold in a specific company's shares, there might be a rebound on recovery hopes and/or takeover bids. But (and this is difficult) even if you have not sold early, do not hang on to a deteriorating investment, unless there are signs of a regeneration of growth, perhaps from a new area of the business.

The dynamics that lead to a decline in growth are either specific to a given business or to the industry in which it operates. Try to distinguish which has hit your company. If the decline is due to a negative change in the sector rather than bad management, you should stay invested long enough to allow for remedial action.

The company might reverse the decline in future sales and profits by a strategic merger, or by concentrating greater resources in a new horizon of growth within its business. In short, if you do not believe the company's best days are behind it but are yet to come, do not sell its shares, even if in the short term they suffer from negative dynamics. Only sell if you no longer believe the future prospects of the business are sure, or as attractive.

If the deterioration in the business stems from stale and complacent management, you ought to think about selling. Look for the signs that management has become self-serving, greedy and has lost sight of its essential role of trusteeship for the assets of its shareholders. When you see them, the only rational action is to sell that company's shares and to invest the proceeds in a better opportunity or in more of your winning shares.

Corporate decadence
Excessive executive compensation and incentive packages – especially

when the company is doing badly – can be an indication of corporate decadence that might prompt you to sell. Notably, if companies lower the price of the stock options awarded to their top executives after a fall in the market, they are not worthy long term business partners. I should seriously consider selling their shares. Their executives benefit from an unfair win–win deal, which cannot be said to correspond with the interests of shareholders.

When a company moves from cost-efficient and utilitarian premises to new ostentatious headquarters, beware. Such *largesse* with shareholders' money can indicate decadence at the top and loss of concentration on shareholder value. If such a move can be justified on purely commercial grounds, fine; but in many cases it is a sign of fuzzy and wasteful thinking that can affect business judgement and major decisions.

Waste pervades a company's culture. It indicates that those at the top are no longer in touch with the reality of their responsibilities. Self-promotion and/or pursuit of personal agendas, a lack of clarity in strategy and defined goals, serial strategic 'reviews', courtesy of expensive management consultants, to identify problems and find solutions – these can all be signals to sell. If management has lost its way and is floundering, the business lacks leadership. The shares should probably be sold.

A better opportunity

If you can afford regularly to pump fresh funds into your share portfolio, your investment fund will compound and grow faster. Realistically however, this option is not available to many of us. When a wonderful investment opportunity presents itself, the solution is to sell something. Look carefully at all your shares before you decide which position to liquidate in order to invest the money in shares of the new more promising company. This is a hard call.

After all, if one of your shares has under-performed for fundamental reasons, as described above, you should have long since disposed of it. If not, then you would be selling a good business in order to buy one which you believe to be a better one. You will need to be sure of your facts on the prospects of both companies before you decide whether it is worth risking selling something good, and probably paying tax, to buy something which you hope might prove even better.

Harvest capital gains tax free each year

The pursuit of wealth should not just be for material gain. Money can also enhance other aspects of your life. It can buy you time for yourself, for your family and for your friends. Do not cut back your investment fund just to take advantage of tax breaks and bank the profits. That would be financially unsound and spiritually quite sad. But do use some of your profit each year to 'invest' in enhanced quality of life: use the money to travel, to learn or to help others. Harvest just enough each year to use your tax exemptions and enjoy both the material and 'feel good' effect of wealth creation, and stay motivated to continue with your plan.

When not to sell

Really the answer to when not to sell is 'most of the time'. Apart from for the reasons outlined earlier, it is invariably better to sit tight and hold on to the shares you have. However, there are a number of instances where you might be tempted to sell for all the wrong reasons.

A pending bear market

After a long bull market run, when shares are high, there could be a sharp correction. It might be triggered by fear of higher inflation and interest rates, or destabilisation in an economy on the other side of the world. But stock market corrections are usually triggered by events not on the radar screen now. Do not sell shares in outstanding businesses because of fear of short term turbulence or a correction. You would only be guessing what the market might do.

An actual bear market

Never sell into a bear market. You would be joining in the madness of the crowd psychology, which is devoid of any rational deliberation. You might sell your shares for a price that subsequently falls further but would you buy the shares back before they rebounded? Almost certainly not. In the meantime you will have resigned your position as part-owner of a great business that will become more valuable one day.

Stick with the best and forget the rest

When at the end of a reasonable gestation period, say ten years or more, you do a tally, you will see that a few extraordinary shares will have earned most of the fortune you have derived from patiently buying and holding good shares through thick and thin. So buy into something good for keeps and do not let short term considerations tempt you to let go.

When the market declines and/or short term investors take profits, it will be gut-wrenching to watch your shares fall, maybe as much as 30 to 50 per cent, but accept this loss of value with equanimity; stay calm and stay resolutely invested. Nothing would have been achieved, in terms of your financial goal, if you had sold your best shares at the recent 'high' or peak price, unless you had also bought them back at a lower price. To have merely 'lightened up' would have been the very opposite of what you are trying to achieve, namely to concentrate as much of your capital as you can in the shares of great businesses. To have 'locked in your profit' (by selling) would have achieved nothing more than short term gain. You would be all the poorer in terms of future wealth creation.

In a raging bull market

Even if your shares soar, and the financial community's argument to 'lighten up' or to 'lock in your profit' seems logical and compelling, stop and think of it in terms of gardening. If you locked in your profit by selling you would be pulling up the healthiest and rarest blooms which year after year will transform your garden from the common to the spectacular. You would be leaving the weeds and plants that are nothing special. Then ask yourself, what could you possibly plant instead with equal, if not more, panache?

As for whether you should sell shares that have soared in order to re-invest in others that have under-performed, it beggars belief that highly paid and intelligent professionals not only frequently advise this nonsense, but also act upon it. Likewise, professional investors' tendency to rotate investments from one sector to another, as if milking cows in a shed, should not be emulated.

That practice may produce short term performance results for the professionals, but it will decimate your future finances, and incur high transactional costs. Meanwhile, if you are lucky, you may be able to buy cast-off 'fallen angels' at reasonable prices after the professionals have (temporarily) dumped them.

To summarise when to sell in one word – don't. That is do *not* sell if you bought the right shares in the first place. Yet the reasons not to sell, summarised at the end of this chapter, are promoted daily as good ideas by the financial community. Such short term advice will damage your future wealth and must be resisted.

Your investment mistakes will obviously damage your future fortunes, so stay out of harm's way and avoid such mistakes rather than try to score short term points against the market. Do not follow the professionals, nor try to beat them. Remain systematic and consistent within your investment strategy and you will attain your financial goal.

Before leaving the subject of selling, take a look at the following situation so as to understand the unsettling emotions and practical problems you would encounter if you allowed yourself to be swept up in a wave of crowd hysteria in the stock markets. Then read on to Step 7 on market psychology – the final, and arguably the most vital, part of your learning curve as a private investor.

What if…?

After heavy falls on Wall Street, Hong Kong and Tokyo overnight, London market makers unceremoniously mark down UK blue chip shares within the FTSE-100 Index.

They do this to protect themselves. They want to deter institutional investors with large lines of stock from dumping shares, thus increasing the risk of losses as the market makers are obliged to take the shares onto their books, even in a falling market, until the buyers come back into the market.

The front page of the *Financial Times* that morning reports the severe correction in world equity markets. An editorial on the leader page, and comment in the Lex column argues that a crash on the world stock markets was long overdue (because of over-valuation on Wall Street). European and London stock markets will not be able to resist selling pressure that day warns the *FT* leader. Lex cannot resist a smug 'we told you so' tone.

BBC Radio 4's *Today* programme, which normally yawns through the 'money news' and gives scant coverage to it compared with political and sports news, kicks off at 6 am with 'The Overnight Crash on World Stock Markets'. The BBC correspondent is in the dealing room of a top investment bank in the City. He interviews its head of equities who predicts the market will open 5 per cent or even 10 per cent lower, wiping billions off the value of shares. Someone says 'meltdown'. You gulp down your porridge and ring Giles, your stockbroker.

It is now 7.10 am. The phone keeps ringing: his voice mail is not switched on. At 8.20 am you ring him again. It is hard to get through, but eventually someone tells you Giles is on the phone. You stay on the line. Several minutes later you ring his mobile. He picks it up, irritated, and quotes his on-screen pre-opening share prices. You can hardly believe the falls – even before trading has started.

Giles asks you what you want to do. Blue chip technology companies that were rated a 'buy' last week, now look ugly, having shed 25 per cent in value within minutes of the opening bell. You start to panic. You ask him whether you should sell. He is unlikely to deter you. You could be proved right – short term. Or you could be wrong. Both ways, he makes a commission only if you *do something*.

At this stage, volume is still very low. The institutions are sitting on the sidelines, watching their screens. If prices fall low enough, they will buy. For now, they are happy to watch the little guys go out in the field and get slaughtered. You decide to sell because you imagine that the meltdown has already begun, and you want to protect what profit you still have on your shares by liquidating them.

You vaguely vow to buy them back cheaper. But you are not really thinking at all, just reacting emotionally and impulsively to powerful suggestions all around you. Your broker sells your shares at a large discount. You take a hit from the spreads between buying and selling price as well as the market decline.

You go to work. It is 8.40 am and you are running late. A few hours on the market calms down. Wall Street opens firmer, and European bourses regain their composure. Prices stop falling. They start to rise. Wall Street rallies. London rises strongly in response. The professionals are in the market now – buying *your* shares at cheaper prices.

You are at work so you cannot easily check up on the market or deal. The stock market in London closes at 4.30 pm, ten points higher than yesterday, in anticipation of a strong close on Wall Street. Your shares are worth 8 per cent less than they were yesterday and 14 per cent more than you got for them this morning. But you are loathe to re-purchase them (at a loss) in the morning. You would take another hit on the spreads. You could also be exposed to further market volatility, which in your present state of mind you perceive as risk.

But you know, when you are thinking rationally, that over the long term, the greater risk is in selling a good investment and being out of the stock market. So the best strategy in volatile markets – whether it be caused by buying-mania or selling-panic – is to do nothing.

To summarise

When to sell
- When you've made a mistake.
- When the business is deteriorating.
- When a better opportunity presents itself.
- When you want to boost your income by harvesting tax relief.

When not to sell
- Speculation that a general market decline is pending.
- Your shares rise sharply, and pundits advise 'take profits'.
- A market correction – when investor psychology has changed from bullish to bearish – but for how long you know not.
- Market disappointment with results – prompting a sharp fall in the value of your shares.
- Analysts downgrade expectations from a company in which you hold shares – because a rival has issued a profits warning.
- Suggestions that your company's share price has 'got ahead of itself', and should be exchanged for those of lower rated rivals which are now 'better value'.

- Sector churning – professional investors take profits in a sector and re-invest in one that has 'not participated' – a euphemism for underperformed.
- Threat or declaration of war. War is inflationary and so erodes the value of cash. So in times of war do not sell your shares to build up your cash.

Step 7

The Psychology of Investment

How to view the manic-depressive mood swings
of the markets with equanimity, cope with greed
and fear, stay calm and resolutely invested

STEP 7

The Psychology of Investment

Investment mistakes

You have to know yourself before you start to invest for the long term. We are all susceptible to recurring investment mistakes that reflect our character, and we saw in Step 2 that investment personality types probably fall into three typical categories. You should have been able to identify yourself in one of them. If we fail to recognise the pattern, we shall neither learn from our mistakes nor devise a method to avoid them. The natural tendency is to discount our past ill-judged decisions as wrong responses to prevailing market conditions and/or random events. But that is a fallacy.

Study your own pattern of investment mistakes, and learn to recognise what triggered the responses/thinking behind those decisions. Examples of common recurring mistakes, with possible interpretation of each, are:

Selling too early – greed

The share in question has performed brilliantly, and greed, rather than fear, prompts you to cash out. You may have been enticed to sell by your stockbroker ('no-one ever went bust taking a profit'). Your initial euphoria at selling for a profit is often quickly replaced by a sense of loss, especially when you count the cost of tax, and if the sold shares then rise.

Selling too early – impatience

Impatience is one of the most damaging character faults in a long term investor. It may cause you to behave irrationally and unpredictably, which in a buy-and-hold strategy is dangerous. You must not expect to reap as soon as you sow. If shares you buy languish, or even if they fall, be patient. Do not sell unless the fundamental reasons that prompted purchase have changed. You will be rewarded as long as you were right in your choice of shares in the first place.

Selling too late – denial

A buy-and-hold strategy is strictly not a 'no brainer': you must monitor the progress of your investments and react promptly if you have made a mistake, or if the business in which you have bought shares has deteriorated and is no longer a good long term growth prospect.

If you are so relaxed as to be negligent, you will lose money, or the opportunity to re-invest better, which amounts to the same thing. Complacency is not the only danger; denial is often the reaction of private investors to bad news.

Don't ask me how or why, but research has shown that if you place a toad into water and heat steadily, the toad will not notice it is beginning to boil until it is too late. So private investors who deny bad news regarding their investments are in danger. Do not confuse negatives affecting the general market with those specific to the company in which you have shares. Only the latter should concern you as a long term private investor.

Underestimating problems in a business/sector – complacency

Healthy suspicion of short term market appraisals/conclusions might lead you to discount early warning signals. This is particularly danger-ous in small to medium-sized businesses where adverse conditions can be overwhelming. That is one reason why you reduce risk by investing only in large capitalisation companies – they are comparatively resilient.

Hanging on to 'save' tax – bad personal finance management

No-one likes to pay tax. But if a share shows signs of decline, sell it and pay tax on your gains, rather than risk future capital losses. Or if you have already lost money, sell and use your tax loss. Your creed as an investor is to earn the max and pay the tax. Your investment decisions should not be driven by tax considerations.

Trying to finesse prices/market time – love of a bargain and negotiation

We've said it already: it is fatal to try to predict market timing. However, most investors have at some time or other identified a fine business with excellent prospects, but when told its shares were priced at X have doggedly tried to buy them for X minus Y. Or they have tried to sell shares above market price and risked not selling, or selling for much less. That is not rational investment policy.

Market timing leads investors to buy or sell a share *price* as opposed to buying or selling shares in a *business*. Do not try to finesse market prices. If a business looks promising and you can afford to buy its shares and hold on to them for several years, then pay the market price and invest in future prosperity.

This wealth creation strategy is risk-reduced. But still it is not for nervous investors who psychologically cannot tolerate market turbulence and share price volatility. It is for resilient, optimistic people who believe that common sense, basic knowledge and persistence in buying shares in great businesses will in due course transform their financial destiny.

Resist the urge to join in the madness of crowds

Hans Tietmeyer, the Bundesbank's representative in the European Central Bank, said, in January 1999, that monetary policy should not be interventionist. He argued that cutting interest rates can easily send the wrong message and lead to investment mistakes and inflated asset prices: 'This would tend to move financial markets in the direction of casino capitalism.'

Herr Tietmeyer spoke after the US Federal Reserve Board had cut rates in response to what the chairman of the Fed, Alan Greenspan, characterised as 'an abrupt stringency in financial markets' during autumn 1998.

Greenspan insisted, 'We were not attempting to prop up equity prices, nor did we plan to continue to cut rates until equity prices recovered, as some have erroneously inferred … Our objective is the maximum sustainable growth of the US economy, not particular levels of asset prices.'

Whatever Mr Greenspan's objective, his deft touch did much to restore investor confidence worldwide, and share prices duly recovered. Changes in interest rates, up or down, can transform investor psychology almost as fast as the spin of a roulette wheel.

When the cost of money falls, there is less incentive for investors to hold cash on deposit, and more inclination to take greater risk for better returns via bonds, shares or property. Cheaper money allows businesses to grow faster, so is good for shares. Conversely, when money becomes dearer, there is usually a sell-off in bonds (gilts) and shares. Property values are also hit. Investor psychology turns bearish when rates rise because the risk/reward ratio then favours holding more cash. Such responses, however rational in the short term, should not faze you unduly.

If you have bought shares in efficient growth businesses and/or good quality property, you must resist the urge to cut and run when fear is in the air. Also resist the urge to join in the madness of the crowds when irrational exuberance abounds. You cannot afford to become a 'casino capitalist'.

Gambling can be exhilarating. But the wealth creation strategy out-

lined here is based on a steadfast and consistent long term commitment. Think of the shares or property you buy as businesses with excellent prospects over several years – they are not bets on a quick profit.

The buy-and-hold strategy takes patience – and guts

There will be times when your shares will become depressed in price –
that reality is inherent in the nature of the stock market. But do not let
market declines depress you. Or, the value of property might fall during an economic slowdown, but as long as your property yields enough
to cover the cost of financing it, and you have staying power, you can
sustain the downturn. So do not sell, but hold on.

When share prices or the value of property falls, take the opportunity to buy more shares in wonderful businesses or first class property at
lower prices. It will not be easy to stay calm when all around you are
losing their heads so now we confront the difficult psychological
aspects of committing yourself to a long term wealth creation strategy.
Your mentality, confidence and (good) behaviour as an investor are crucial to success in wealth creation.

Why good investor behaviour rules work better than slide rules

Aspects of my investment strategy might be called 'rules'. But successful investment in shares does not lend itself to *absolute* rules. If it did,
there would be no losers, only winners. So much depends on intangi-
bles, such as mass psychology and random events yet to happen.

For example, the 'Asian contagion' spread to share markets in the
western world after South East Asian markets crashed in late 1997. But
by the summer of 1998 the US and European stock markets recovered

and reached new peaks. In early autumn Russia defaulted and the near collapse of the hedge fund, Long Term Capital Management, led to serious dislocations. The markets spiralled downwards. But a few weeks later they were again at record highs.

Events that move markets are usually unpredictable. You cannot influence or change what might happen, so stop worrying. Simply set yourself a realistic goal, carefully select which shares, funds or property to buy, then buy and hold them until you have achieved your objective. Only by sticking to your gameplan can you resist the psychological pressures to react to short term market changes.

That is why 'rules' of conduct will help you to succeed in the money game. They will liberate you from the advice industry's myopic focus. You can stay calm, and manage your investments rationally and systematically and for the greatest possible capital gain.

The 'rules' of good investor behaviour after investment are:

- Do not sell what you like just because the market says so.
- Do not follow the crowd into a hyped sector out of mania/greed.
- Admit any mistakes, and take appropriate action – it is therapeutic.
- Review regularly the reasons why you invested and ensure they are still valid.
- Make fewer decisions, but with greater conviction.
- Do not agonise about what you missed.

Buying and selling shares tests character and courage as much as judgement

Volatility in the markets is uncomfortable. It demands self-control and counter-intuitive responses on your part. When skiing, you are safe if you lean towards the valley, even at great height, and on a steep slope, but you will lose balance and risk falling if you give in to the natural instinct of wanting to cling to the mountain. So as an investor in shares do not let stock market jitters faze you. Keep the faith in your rational, methodical investment plan, and stay invested. Even in a bear market, just grin and bear it.

The stock market is manic-depressive – do not let it affect your moods

Do not under-estimate the power of the market to move you emotionally. In a study on anti-depressants published in March 1999, Merrill Lynch noted that some of the fifty physicians questioned believed their caseloads would not increase over the next three years – not least because 'people are happier now as a result of a good economy'. Maybe in a bear market, we should all buy shares in drug companies: Eli Lilly (Prozac), Pfizer (Zoloft) and SmithKline Beecham (Paxil). They sold over $6 billion worth of their anti-depressants in 1998 (even when the market was up).

The activities of traders, private or professional, has increased volatility in the share markets and exacerbated the impression that they are casinos. The stock market, particularly in New York, has the liquidity and mechanisms to handle this activity, but day trading is not recommended for investors intent on a risk-reduced strategy for maximum growth.

Stock markets are not casinos, but capital markets

Businesses raise cheap, long term money to finance expansion and growth via the stock market. Yet short term trading gives the market a dangerous casino-like aura. But you do not have to follow market mentality. Stay locked into something good, and you should earn superior returns in good time.

When stock markets are at record levels, the risk of falls is greater. But do not freeze with fear and do nothing. Buy shares via a systematic, staggered programme over, say, a year. That will take the guesswork out of market timing, and allow you to average out the cost of shares you buy (see Step 5).

You might feel that psychologically, the only way you will stick to a long term plan is to engage a financial adviser to keep you on track. That would be the equivalent of having a personal trainer call on you at 8 am each morning to ensure you take exercise to attain and maintain physical fitness. No number of personal advisers can help you become fit, whether physically or financially, if you are not motivated and do not have confidence in your strategy. You just would not stay the course.

Make sure your expectations are realistic

If your expectations are too high, you might put too little into your investment fund, and fall short of your goal. Or you will be disappointed and lose faith and sight of your ultimate goal. Moreover, expectations of unrealistically high returns in too short a period of time will put you in panic mode whenever the market falls. Instead of rejoicing in your distance *from* the market, you would be running with the crowd. When you fall in step *with* the market, you abandon the rules of behaviour conducive to investment success. You become susceptible not just to panic attacks that might prompt selling, but also to manic impulses to buy. Your decisions are the market's decisions. You are on an emotional roller-coaster, gripped by the highly contagious, and wealth threatening, crowd psychology which prevails in the market.

Stay cool within a realistic time frame

The longer your time frame, the less important short term fluctuations in value will be, although your emotions will be affected. Your plan should give you confidence that you know what you are doing, and why you are doing it. Then you will withstand market setbacks without panic.

Know your own risk tolerance

You need behavioural rules to guard you from harm, whether psychological or financial. Risk tolerance is perceived as both the psychological ability to accept risk and the material means to withstand risk. But essentially it should be a rational response to what you are trying to achieve. Risk tolerance is not a measure of your *machismo*. Nor is it necessarily commensurate with material means.

Witness the fact that the very wealthy tend to be highly risk averse, because they have more to lose. In reality, they can afford to lose capital, and so logically they could adopt an aggressive investment plan, but psychologically, the wealthy are conservative – they just want to hang on to what they have rather than risk any of it by trying to accumulate more.

Needy people on the other hand, will often take irrational risks out of desperation to make money. Look at all those who pile into betting shops on weekday afternoons, or who bet a high proportion of their weekly income on the lottery or on football pools. They can barely afford to lose, yet the odds are that they will.

Gambling may be in your genes

Analyse yourself before you start to analyse balance sheets. If you feel unduly constrained by this philosophy of investment in shares only within a narrow range of businesses, maybe you are a person who enjoys taking risks. You might derive stimulation and fun from gambling in shares while at the same time investing in a separate fund for the longer term. A little gambling might be a good thing – if it keeps you motivated and enthusiastic. You should enjoy yourself, as well as profit from investing.

But recognise that speculation in shares is like playing with fireworks: the effect can be spectacular, but if the things go off in your hands, you would be lucky to escape without serious damage to your capital and confidence – both of which will affect you negatively as an investor.

Try to understand why you feel drawn to speculate. Is it greed, or the thrill of living dangerously? Gamblers are compulsive and are addicts. Watch people playing roulette and witness what is essentially a self-destructive activity. When they win, they slap the chips around the table to win more. When they lose, they pile on even more chips to try to recoup their losses. It is the roller-coaster ride of emotion, whether up or down, to which they are addicted.

The excitement is all-consuming, but to some it is a destructive drug. The danger from 'experimenting' with short term trading in shares is that it could unsettle you, and spoil your long term plan. Only you can judge whether you can handle a little speculation for fun without it ruining you. If in doubt, leave it out.

My genes probably predispose me to reckless gambling, so I resist any such urge. My childhood memories are of my parents all dressed up to go either to after-dinner card parties or to have friends in to play cards. Their card games would go on until the early hours. The men would play poker and the women canasta.

On the morning after, my sisters and I would tiptoe into the smoke-filled living room and steal salted almonds, dried fruits and chocolates left over from the night before. Coloured chips and cards were strewn across green felt tables, astride full ashtrays. They left everything but money. I would scan the carpet under the tables looking for fallen six-pences, but there was none. The Parents & Co played with folding money.

Set aside a 'mad money fund' – if you must

In this wealth creation strategy you are not gambling and you won't be expecting to make a quick buck. But if you are likely to become bored you may need a little excitement to motivate you to stick with your long term strategy. Set aside a small fund for pure speculation. Keep your 'mad money fund' in a separate account. Do not let it exceed 5 per cent of your total free funds.

Back your hunches; invest in short term market trends, or even buy into some of the 'taboo' categories listed in Step 5, such as special situations. You could 'day trade' online, or buy and sell through a discount broker. But never invest, let alone gamble, in the stock market with borrowed money. If you lose 15 per cent on a speculative position, immediately sell it and use your tax losses. Harvest any profits, so that only your original capital – that 5 per cent of free funds – is in all that is in your mad money fund.

Online trading and day trading

Buying and selling over the Internet allows you to deal for far less, and virtually on the same footing in terms of instant access and information as a professional investor. Use only a leading online broker. You can get quality company and industry research and daily market commentary on screen, as well as good execution. If you buy and sell on a rolling settlement, i.e. day trade or invest short term, you would pay for losses, or receive a cheque for gains within a few days. But as a beginner you should beware. You could so easily fall into the trap of trying to beat the market with frequent trading which, at whatever discounted price, is not normally a profitable exercise. The market is manic-depressive and the resulting volatility in share prices can greatly affect you psychologically if you are plugged into it minute-by-minute on a daily basis. You could end up losing self-control – and a lot of money – by slipping out of investment mode and into gambling online.

When, instead, you have to reach a stockbroker on the phone before you can deal, you have more time (often lots more time) to reflect before reacting to market movements. You might still make an investment mistake, but not before weighing up the odds.

The temptation to trade/gamble beyond your means online is very great. A wise investor, particularly one that may be rattled by the market, slows down, asks questions and obtains written information before reaching a rational investment decision. That decision-making process is speeded up online, so you are in more danger of making mistakes. The risks are even greater if you are not sure what shares to buy. As a beginner, you ought perhaps to start investing via an advisory, or execution-only broker until you have the knowledge and confidence to deal online.

Moreover, cyberspace is full of con men and fraudsters using new technology to play old tricks to cheat naïve investors with promises of quick profits. So never rely on what you read online to make an investment decision. Do your homework.

Why doing your own thinking will keep you safe from the madness of crowds

This strategy liberates you from the prevailing wisdom and the methods used by professional fund managers. So do your own thinking and be wary of recommendations of brokers' analysts. It can elate or deflate you – even scare you. But for all their detailed knowledge, analysts are under pressure to take a fairly short term view. They must produce 'stories' which their colleagues on the equity sales desks can use to generate commissions via sell or buy orders. Analysts also tend to fall in love with sectors, and then argue that they are more exciting than perhaps they are in reality.

As Warren Buffett said when a textile company finally turned in a modest profit after years, a horse that counts to ten is a clever horse but it is not a brilliant mathematician. Buffett has skilfully projected a deceptively innocent 'country boy' image to Wall Street from his base in Omaha, Nebraska. His annual statements to shareholders of Berkshire Hathaway are a study course in wealth creation. He argues that short term forecasts may tell you a lot about the forecaster but nothing about the future.

The media exacerbates the manic-depressive moods of the market

The media also plays a powerful role in influencing market psychology, and in the perception of specific sectors or businesses. After all, it's an auction market, driven by mass psychology, which can quickly turn to mass hysteria, whether in a bull market or in a bear sell-off.

In a bull market, the media hardly dares call a market downturn, and tends to join in the **hubris** and hype. But at the first sign of a crack in market confidence, emotive phrases such as 'market meltdown', '1930s-type slump' and 'asset bubble', enter media speak and fear pervades the markets. Pessimism or optimism in the stock market are self-fulfilling short term.

The trouble with the media is it wants black and white answers, and ever-faster responses to issues that are often short term and can distort the 'big picture' from a long term investor's perspective. Media focus on the here and now can sometimes deepen short term misconceptions in the market.

If you grow smug and bore friends about your shares – seek help

When you feel really good, almost smug, about the performance of your investments, and you start to bore friends with stories of your derring-do in the stock market, seek advice. You may have become susceptible to market hype, self-delusion and the madness of crowds. You may have forgotten the rules on risk reduction, and started to let mass hysteria in the market decide what, and when, you buy or sell.

Control your natural impulse to run with the crowd out of fear or greed, and think for yourself. You can thus tolerate, even capitalise on, price volatility over many years without undue stress, or deviation from your sensible plan to make money. You cannot avoid ups and downs in the stock market. So understand, and learn to cope with, your psychological responses to market risk and price volatility.

The key is to put your money out to work on specific, attainable goals to meet your financial needs. If you maintain confidence in your plan, you are less likely to be deflected from it. You know you can grow wealth by investing in good quality businesses via shares and/or buying quality property, but often it is a psychological response, not a reason, which prompts you to buy or sell what you ought not to.

The rules of wealth creation

That is why you absolutely need to adhere to a strict and coherent strategy when buying and selling shares, such as that outlined here. The rules are not designed to help you beat the stock market in the short term; they reduce your risk and resolve four difficulties that confront us private investors in the stock market:

1. How to identify exceptional businesses whose shares are likely to increase many-fold over a decade or so
As I have stressed, the key to reduced risk/maximum returns from shares is to buy *only*:
- Shares in businesses you understand.
- Shares in growth businesses with the resilience to withstand an economic slump.
- Shares in companies that are not just defensive, but also positioned to go on the offensive and grow above average when the economy accelerates.

2. How to control irrational impulses during the long holding period
Controlling irrational impulses and avoiding temptation, is also crucial to success. Ulysses tied himself to a mast so as not to be tempted by siren voices which might steer him off course – a rational response to overcoming temptation that is prevalent and pervasive.

My system puts you out of harm's way, in a time zone further out in the future than the rest of the market. If your time horizon is long and your expectations of the pace of growth realistic, you will not feel in danger and compelled to keep changing strategy. The feeling that you are in trouble is one that you must avoid so as not to lapse into irrational, erratic behaviour leading to investment mistakes.

We have all experienced changes in our normal behaviour when under the influence of crowd psychology, whether at a football match or in the global response to the sad death of Diana, Princess of Wales. Almost without realising it, you can lose a sense of personal responsibility and control, and become affected by pervasive, rapid and random mood swings as dictated by the masses.

Just as you might drive recklessly in order to get to your destination in an unrealistically short amount of time, so the feeling that you are not on track to reach your financial goal on time may prompt you to take extra risks in your investment decisions. You are less likely to succumb to these lapses of reason if you stick to this strategy and so distance yourself from the emotional dangers in the market.

3. When to buy and when to sell, or when not to
According to this strategy you would not attempt to buy shares cheap or sell them high. You would concentrate not on when, but on which shares, to buy and why – and which to sell.

You would buy shares in well-managed businesses with great future prospects. Then, just as you would not call up a surveyor to value your house each day, you would not look too often at the price of your shares.

Your success will depend on your patience and persistence. You must stay invested. Private investors (and some highly paid fund managers) often lose money selling good shares on impulse, emotion and/or bad logic. They then compound their errors by dithering over when, and in what, to re-invest the proceeds. The psychological effect of this wrong-footedness is highly damaging because you are unlikely to reverse a mistake with a correct decision; you are more likely to follow up such a mistake with another, similar one.

4. How to manage money in practical terms, given limited time and information
The fourth difficulty in buying shares is a practical one. You may be in

full-time employment and/or not inclined to spend hours studying companies. You are in an information vacuum compared with professional investors. But the professionals all get the same information at the same time, and, accordingly, often deal at the same time in the same direction. So the information explosion has not resulted in orderly markets but greater volatility.

Share prices reflect the financial community's appraisals right now. But the market does not always see the wood from the trees. So short term price movements are random and often irrational. In these circumstances you, the private investor, are at a distinct advantage. You can ignore short term appraisals and buy shares in enterprises with promising future growth.

You do not need minute-by-minute information from the global stock markets. This strategy relies on your informed good judgement. Once you have invested, the plan requires low maintenance. You do not need to spend hours on your investments each week. On the contrary, pursue your other hobbies and interests, and get out and about – be aware as a consumer, ask questions and notice changes. Buy shares in a few carefully chosen businesses or good property. Then you need only monitor progress once or twice a year. Unless there is deterioration in the prospects of any given investment, you need take no further action.

Finally

My strategy will work because it will get you into the market with confidence, irrespective of at what level, or at what point in the business cycle the economy happens to be. Stock markets move in a random manner. Unless you are invested during the major upswings, your overall capital gain will be limited. You simply cannot afford to be out of the stock market if you plan to grow your capital and your income over the next five, ten or fifteen years.

Only rare businesses meet the investment criteria set out in this strategy, so your choices, being limited, are relatively simple. As Warren Buffett argues:

'To invest successfully, you need not understand beta, efficient markets, modern portfolio theory, option pricing or emerging markets. You may, in fact, be better off knowing nothing of these. Your goal as an investor should simply be to purchase, at a rational price, a part interest in an easily understandable business whose earnings are virtually certain to be materially higher five, ten, and twenty years from now.'

In other words, use common sense to buy shares or property and have the patience, persistence and staying power to hold them until they produce the powerful profit that creates real wealth.

Good luck.

Who's Who and What's What

ADRs: American Depository Receipts are certificates allowing American citizens to buy foreign shares priced in US dollars.

Advanced corporation tax: A prepayment of a company's corporation tax, levied when dividends are paid. Shareholders used to receive a 20 per cent tax credit to show that tax had been paid out of companies' earnings. Standard rate tax payers did not pay any more tax and non-tax payers could reclaim the tax. But that tax credit was abolished, except for PEPs and ISAs where it was reduced from 20 to 10 per cent in 1999/2000, and is due to be scrapped entirely in April 2004.

Alpha, Beta, Gamma, Delta: Blue chip shares are classified as Alphas, the next 500 Betas, and the rest Gammas and Deltas. You don't really need to know this as it is a distraction from your task, which is to identify and buy only extraordinary Alphas, which get an A for performance.

Analyst: A specialist who studies facts, figures and background of economies, industries and specific companies to make recommendations to investment banks, brokerage houses, investment managers or private investors on what securities or currencies to buy and to sell, and when. Research is invaluable to professionals who need an immediate view, but private investors with a long term perspective do not necessarily need to read it.

Annual percentage rate: This is the rate you pay for credit (borrowing) each year, expressed as a percentage. For example, if you borrow

£1,000 at 17 per cent APR you will pay £170 a year for the privilege. Any consumer loan agreement will be subject to an agreed APR (which includes the lender's fees). Some confused borrowers calculate that double digit APR rates are more advantageous than single digit ones. But APR is your cost and the lender's gain. Compulsive users of credit and store cards should consolidate their debts into a single card with the lowest APR (and then repay their debt).

Annual report: This is a document produced by companies, which is legally required to be sent out to all shareholders prior to the annual general meeting. It contains the financial results, dividends to be paid, the profit and loss account, the balance sheet, reports on progress of operations in the past twelve months and prospects over the next year. Proxy forms are included so that you can vote on resolutions to be raised at the AGM even if you do not attend. It is indirectly a 'sales document' for the company's shares as it presents the information in the best possible light. Bar charts showing past records of earnings/dividends and share price growth are often included along with glossy photographs of products and top people. Pay, bonuses and options granted to executive board directors are stated, and their shareholdings listed. The accounts in the annual report must be signed off by the company's auditors as giving a true and fair view of its (current) state of affairs (qualifications to that seal of approval are bad news). This is a snapshot of a company, taken up to some three months before publication. In industries highly sensitive to changes in consumer/investor psychology or interest rates, such as brokerage or investment banking, the annual report can be out of date by the time it is despatched to shareholders.

Annuity: An annual income for the rest of your life. It is paid by life insurance companies in exchange for a lump sum of capital. Annuity rates depend on age, state of health and long term bond yields. The elderly, or those with proven below-average life expectancy, for example smokers, receive higher annuities than everybody else. Annuities must be purchased by retired people with personal pensions by the time they reach seventy-five. Once you buy an annuity you cannot switch out of it: you are locked into the income it provides for the rest of your life. There are various types of annuities: the most commonly purchased by the retired is an immediate annuity. The other types include deferred, temporary, certain, guaranteed, joint life and last survivor, escalating, variable, investment-linked and capital-protected.

Arbitrage: To take a position that capitalises on a temporary price abnormality. Risk arbitrageurs bet one way or another on whether a takeover bid will materialise. The arbs make a killing when they can marshal enough shares to force a higher offer.

Asset backed investment: An investment linked to the value of shares, bonds and property.

AVCs: Additional Voluntary Contributions to a pension scheme, which a member chooses to pay in addition to normal contributions, if any, to secure extra benefit.

Back-end load: Charge paid on sale or surrender of an investment in a unit trust or other collective fund. Only relates to collective funds.

Base price: The price used for purposes of calculating capital gains or losses when selling securities. For example, if the base price is £10 and you sell for £18, you will be liable to pay capital gains tax on your profit of £8. If on the other hand you bought at £18 and sold at £10, you would crystallise a capital loss of £8 that you could offset against capital gains from your more successful investments.

Base Rate: The interest rate fixed by the Bank of England (independent of Government) which is the rate at which the Bank of England will lend to other banks. Base Rate sets the benchmark for bank loans for all borrowers.

Basis price: The price of a share given only as a guide, not as a firm dealing price.

Bear: An investor who is pessimistic about the general market or a specific sector or stock, and accordingly sells in anticipation that prices will fall; or he does not invest pending the expected fall. 'Bearish' denotes this state of pessimism (which in some is a permanent state of mind). Bears sound more rational than bulls. But bears are gripped by fear just as irrational as the greed which prompts bulls to charge into the market.

Bear market: A period of time when sellers outnumber buyers (bears outnumber bulls), or buyers simply retire to the sidelines in antici-pation of adverse or deteriorating economic conditions in general, or in specific sectors or businesses. Accordingly, prices fall.

Beneficiary: The person who receives an inheritance or collects the proceeds from a life insurance policy or an annuity or is the party for whom a trust has been set up to benefit, or for whom a letter of credit has been drawn up.

Bid price: The market price to a seller of directly held shares or shares/units in collective funds. The offer price is the price you pay when you buy. It may include front-end loaded management fees, and/or dealers' spreads. The spread between bid and offer prices when buying and selling securities, either directly or though funds, is wider for small private investors than for institutions buying in bulk. Ask your broker what the spreads are in any given stock for a buyer and for a seller before revealing your own position, and then give him an order. You should argue for a narrow spread.

Block: This denotes the lot, or number of shares or bonds traded or held. Investment bankers 'block trade' large lines of shares or bonds on behalf of their institutional clients.

Blue chip shares: Shares in an established business with a sound track record for profit, growth in earnings, payment of dividends and good management. These are the princes of the stock market and often command higher valuations than the pretenders because of their perceived superior quality and the lower risk of capital loss. In certain circumstances, such as a general market decline, or new com-petitive pressures in specific industries, blue chip shares can fall to the status of 'fallen angels'.

Bond: A security that is equivalent to a loan on the part of the bond holder and a loan being sold on the part of the borrower. Companies and governments issue bonds to borrow money from investors. The Government also issues bonds that offer returns linked to inflation, i.e. index-linked gilts. Bonds pay a fixed or floating rate of interest. If the bond is a fixed-rate bond, the price of the bond, and consequently its yield, are influenced by prevailing interest rates. If floating rate, the interest rate is recalculated at set periods. If convertible, it can be exchanged for shares of the issuer at a pre-fixed conversion price.

Bond rating: A 'score', such as AAA for the best and D for the worst, given by independent rating agencies such as Moody's and Standard & Poor's to bonds, insurance companies or obligations according to their credit-worthiness and the risk of default of the bond issuer (i.e. failure to pay back the bond holder in full with interest). The ratings are regularly reviewed and monitored to reflect new debts or changes in the risk profile, and perceptions of the quality of the issuer.

Bottom fisher: An investor who looks for securities whose price has bottomed out. Can be a lucrative strategy (but cheapness of itself is no reason to buy).

Bottom line: An American term meaning net profit. Often misused to mean 'the last word'.

Bottomed out: A security, market or market sector deemed to have hit its lowest point in price. The implication is that investments are set to rise in future once they have bottomed out.

Bottom up: An approach in securities analysis that looks in detail firstly at a specific company or industry sector and, secondly, at the wider economic and competitive environment in which the proposed investment operates. In short, bottom up is picking shares. Top down is asset allocation on macro-considerations prior to finding the shares. Picking shares is the only rational approach for private investors who are limited in their access to detailed company research, and who cannot monitor the macro-economic factors (GDP growth, inflation, currency) and technical factors (e.g. flow of funds) that might affect their investments in the short term.

Breakage costs: The penalty claimed by a lender if you pay back your loan early.

Breakage profits: The profit the lender might make by re-investing the capital you pay back early.

Break-up value: The sum of the parts of a business were it to be broken up and sold off piece-meal.

Broker: An intermediary who executes the sale or purchase of a security, or brings together buyer and seller in a transaction.

Buffett, Warren: The billionaire investor, also known as the Sage of Omaha. Buffett has skilfully projected a deceptively innocent 'country boy' image from his base in Omaha, Nebraska. But the annual reports of his investment vehicle, Berkshire Hathaway, whose portfolio includes core holdings in Coca-Cola, Gillette and insurance, are a study course in good investment management. A believer in the buy-and-hold strategy, Buffett maintains that while short term forecasts may tell you a lot about the forecaster, they tell you nothing about the future. His message is: do your own thinking, and invest only in businesses within your comprehension.

Bull: The counterpart of the bear. The bull is confident and optimistic and so invests in certain securities, or the market as a whole, in anticipation of a rise in price. Bullish investors expect to make future profits while the bearish fear a decline in the value of their holdings, and capital loss. Bulls can panic too: buying panics distort prices temporarily as do selling panics.

Bull market: A period of time when investors are confident, and prices in the market continue to rise, often in high-volume trading, with 'easy money', i.e. low interest rates pumping high levels of liquidity (i.e. cash) into shares. But bull markets can also occur without these conditions, as long as confidence is high. The securities market is an auction market: for every bullish buyer there is a bearish seller. The former believes he is buying cheap, the latter thinks he is selling high or may need the cash.

Business cycle: The boom/bust cycle which starts with a period of expansion, declining unemployment, rising demand and maybe also rising inflation. This overheating has to be curbed by higher interest rates which in turn lead to a downturn in demand, hence lower business activity, slower growth (even a 'technical recession' – negative growth for two quarters), job cuts and lower prices for goods, services and commodities. Recovery then normally resumes quite rapidly.

Buy-and-hold: A philosophy of investing in securities, essentially in shares, that assumes a long holding period of say five or ten years (or even longer), after purchase. This strategy transcends short term turbulence in the markets and aims to build maximum capital growth and rising income flow over several years.

Buying on margin: This is buying securities with borrowed money lent by the brokerage firm or a bank through which the shares or bonds are purchased. The investor puts up some of the purchase cost (normally 50 per cent) and the lender the rest. The broker/banker charges the investor interest on the loan. The broker holds the said securities in 'street name' and has the right to sell them if their value falls and the loan is not adequately covered with more cash from the investor. Do not do this. It is effectively borrowing short to lend long.

By tender: Would-be buyers are approached by agents and invited to put in offers.

Capital gain/loss: The profit or loss made when a security or property is sold. You pay capital gains tax on the profit after exemption. The highest rate is 40 per cent. In 1999/2000 the tax-free exemption was £7,100. If you sell shares at a loss, you can offset that amount against capital gains. If you do not use your tax-free CGT allowance in any given year, you will lose it. Capital losses can be carried forward and offset against your future capital gains.

Capital market: A market that trades various securities and issues, be they debt or equities.

Capitalisation: The value of a publicly quoted company on the stock market. Its 'price tag' is derived by multiplying the number of shares outstanding by its current share price. For example a company with one billion shares which is quoted at £5 would be capitalised at £5 billion. See also scrip issues.

Capitalism: An economic system which involves individuals owning businesses and property and deriving, and keeping for themselves, profits and wealth accruing from these assets. The State shares in the spoils from private ownership of assets via taxes. The capitalist system, even in a mixed economy, relies essentially on individuals' own initiatives and enterprise, and rewards them for success.

Capped and collared mortgage: A variable-rate mortgage which has a fixed upper-rate limit (the cap) and a fixed lower-rate limit (the collar). It allows you to budget in advance for the maximum and the minimum you might pay in monthly mortgage payments. It limits your risk in the event of sharp rises in interest rates, but when rates fall, the 'collar' can lock you into an above-market cost of borrowing.

Cash dividends: The payment made by a company to its shareholders, usually quarterly or bi-annually.

Churning: Serial trading of securities on behalf of a client in order, primarily, to generate high volume in fees and commissions. The cost of excessive trading erodes capital profits from your investments. Even if you come out of the churning process ahead, question your broker's actions. Your broker cannot act without your consent unless he has your power of attorney and/or is managing your money on a discretionary basis.

Closed-end fund: A fund with a finite number of shares (like a company) which fluctuate in price according to supply and demand. Investment trusts are 'closed-ended' and when demand for their shares falls, they can trade at a discount to the value of their underlying assets.

Common stock or ordinary shares, or equities: All these terms describe a share or a unit of ownership in a publicly quoted company. Shares can be bought and sold on the stock market and their price fluctuates according to the majority of investors' views of their prospects, so leading to capital profits or loss. Shareholders usually have voting rights. Shareholders are part-owners and, as such, can lose their money if the company fails.

Compliance: A set of mandatory regulations designed to ensure honest and transparent transactions on the Stock Exchange or at any member firm or investment management firm. All members of the Stock Exchange and/or authorised firms who give financial advice to clients, and execute transactions on their behalf, must have a compliance officer (and often legal advisers too) to oversee compliance and to deal appropriately with any client complaints or employee misdemeanours. Draconian compliance rules often prevail in global investment banks. In the US, the Stock Exchange is regulated by a statutory body, the SEC. In the UK, the Financial Services Authority has great powers, along SEC lines.

Contrarian investor philosophy: This is essentially contra-think that does not accept prevailing trends and conventional wisdom in the market. The contrarian bets against the prevailing trend in the market in the hope that he or she will profit when current trends revert to his/her way of thinking.

Corporate bond: A debt security issued by a company which promises to pay investors regular interest and the entire nominal price at the redemption date specified at the time of purchase. The price of the bond and its 'yield' fluctuates with prevailing interest rates.

Correction: A pull back in the upward trend of the market, certain sector or specific stocks after a period of uninterrupted rise. A correction does not necessarily herald a crash. It can prove a pause that refreshes when overvalued securities are corrected to lower price levels at which they become attractive to new investors.

Cost basis: The price at which an asset was purchased, or valued in the case of an inherited asset.

Crash: Free fall of securities on capital markets due to investors running for cover of cash as fear overcomes market sentiment. Falling corporate earnings do not often trigger a crash.

Higher interest rates, which dry up the 'liquidity', or cash going into securities, is more likely to cause a stock market crash. The catalyst for a crash is difficult to identify until after the event. Fear is the overriding factor in a crash.

Custodian: An institution or individual who has custody of the securities owned by clients, whether private individuals or institutional.

Cyclical shares: Shares in businesses whose fortunes are linked to the general economy, such as car manufacturing, construction and basic industries.

Deferred annuity: Does not start paying the annuitant until after an agreed length of time.

Deferred-interest mortgage: The interest on the entire loan is only partly paid for an agreed term. But the amount of capital which you must eventually repay increases. This type of mortgage is suitable for someone with reasonable expectations of higher regular income later. It is high risk in that property values could fall, while the amount of your loan effectively increases.

Deflation: Falling prices of goods and services. Is the opposite of inflation and implies a slump and a lifeless economy, even a depression.

Demand deposit: A bank account that allows instant withdrawal without notice or penalty.

Depreciation: In accounting terms, it means the amortisation of the capital costs of fixed assets such as buildings, plant or machinery, purchased by a company in the operation of its business. The scheduled rate of depreciation is offset each year as a deduction against profits, thus effectively reducing the business tax paid by companies and the reported profit. Depreciation also means a decrease in the market value of an asset.

Depression: A protracted recession, also known as a slump. Consumer demand and confidence is depressed and, accordingly, there is a reduction in business activity, rising unemployment and a decline in prices of goods, services and commodities (i.e. deflation).

Derivatives: Financial contracts whose value is essentially derived from an underlying asset. They allow you to take an exposure in relation to an underlying asset without actually owning it, and are thus useful when gearing. There are essentially two kinds of derivatives traded on exchanges:

- **Futures:** Allow you to buy or sell an asset at a specified future date at a fixed price. That price is determined when the contract is agreed.
- **Options:** The right to buy or sell an asset at a specified price on or by a future date. As the name implies, there is no obligation: you can choose to exercise the option, let it expire or sell it to a third party.

Discount: The difference between the lower price a bond or share sells for in the current market and its par value – or asset value. Conversely, a premium reflects a price higher than par or asset value. A premium also means the amount the price of a share is above its issue price in first dealings. Investment trusts can sell for less than their underlying asset value. Property shares go through cycles when they trade at discounts to their net asset value (NAV) and 'conversely' at a different stage of the cycle they command a premium to NAV.

Discount broker: Offers an execution-only service at lower commission. That means he will take your orders and execute them at 'best' prices offered in the market. He does not provide investment advice, research or comforting chatter. For investors who trade frequently and/or know what to buy/sell, discount brokers and online brokers can offer good value.

Discounted mortgages: The normal variable interest rate payable is discounted for a limited period by say 0.5 per cent. The discount can sometimes take the form of a cash discount. Designed to appeal notably to first-time buyers.

Discretionary management: Investments made on behalf of clients without consulting them after they have given a mandate to an investment manager.

Disinflation: Falling inflation. This is healthy for the economy (and for shares) whilst deflation is not. When, for example, interest rates were slashed in the US, Europe and UK in 1998/9, it was because the balance of risk in the world economy was perceived to have shifted from inflation to deflation, due to the deep recession in South East Asia and excessive supply.

Disposable income: Funds available to an individual or institution after all expenses, taxes and obligations, such as debt servicing, have been paid. Consumers spend it; wealth creators invest it, wisely.

Diversification: A philosophy of investing that seeks to mitigate capital loss by spreading risk over a number of different securities and assets. A convenient way to diversify is to invest in shares or collective funds with opposite risks. Concentration in investment can be much more rewarding than heavy diversification. Sixteen different investments will not give you 100 per cent more security than eight. Not having all your eggs in one basket should not lull you into a sense of false security.

Diversified company: Otherwise known as a conglomerate. The company owns and operates diverse businesses (often in basic industrial sectors).

Dividend Re-investment Plan (DRIP): A means by which to compound your shareholding in any given company by opting to have your cash dividend automatically re-invested in more shares, rather than take the cash. Known as scrip dividends in the UK. Most blue chip companies offer this plan free of charge or for a minimal charge. Meticulously retain documents establishing the value of the shares allotted in lieu of cash dividends for future tax purposes, should you decide to sell them later.

Dow Jones Industrial Average: An index of 30 leading American blue chip stocks such as Coca-Cola, Gillette, Merck and American

Express Company, quoted on the New York Stock Exchange. The UK equivalent is the FTSE-100. The Dow is narrow in its range, but is the oldest and most watched stock market index in the western world, as it is perceived as an indicator of global investor confidence. World equity markets take a lead from Wall Street, where the New York Stock Exchange is based. The DJIA is calculated by taking the closing prices of the 30 component companies in any given trading day (and adjusting for stock splits, dividends and mergers) to reach a point count that shows upward or downward trends.

Due diligence: In the strict sense, regarding a property purchase, it means investigation of legals, covenant status, comparable rental levels, quality of location, space, structure, service costs, tax and other aspects of a deal agreed, but subject to contract. In the colloquial sense it means doing your homework prior to making an investment decision.

Duisenberg, Wim: The president of the European Central Bank who presided in January 1999 over the birth of the Euro, initially a sickly currency which, in May 1999, declined sharply in value against the dollar and the pound. Amid calls for ECB intervention to support the single currency, Mr Duisenberg hinted that a weak currency would boost Eurozone trade. He was quoted in the *Times* on 3 June 1999 as saying: 'It's not something we strive for but that [a weak currency] has a beneficial [aspect] cannot be denied.'

Earned income: What you earn at work or selling goods/services. Income tax is due on your earned income, net of deductions and allowances. Unearned income is the profit you make from investments and savings. Tax on unearned (investment) income is added to your earned income and so is effectively levied at your highest rate of tax.

Earnings per share: The amount of profit (after tax) attributable to each ordinary share in a company after all relevant interest and preference dividends have been paid. EPS is calculated by dividing total earnings by the number of outstanding shares.

Endowment: A life insurance product with a savings component that provides a guaranteed sum on death. Investment returns are added via bonuses annually, and at maturity, a terminal bonus is paid. This product is often used as a repayment vehicle for a mortgage, where an interest-only loan has been raised. On death, that loan is automatically repaid. At maturity, the proceeds should, given bonuses, be sufficient to pay off the (mortgage) loan. However, that is not guaranteed. Bonuses are added at the insurance company's discretion. Costs are high, and returns are relatively poor.

Estate: A deceased person's entire wealth in property, financial holdings and other assets.

Ex-dividend (XD) date: Is the dealing deadline after which an investor will not be eligible for the dividend paid approximately two months after. Buy shares before the XD date and you will get the next distribution. Often shares will fall (temporarily) after the XD date is declared, to reflect the loss of dividend.

Federal Reserve Board: Head of central banking system in the US. Set up in 1913. US monetary policy is decided in Washington by the Board of Governors which heads up twelve Federal Reserve banks in different states. The Fed collates and analyses extensive economic data before reaching its decisions. The Fed is equivalent to the Bank of England but carries far more power and influence in world markets. Its mission is to promote sustainable economic growth in the US with negligible inflation. In practice, this has meant changing interest rates to stabilise markets.

Fixed-rate mortgage: A property loan at a fixed rate of interest for an agreed time, subject to penalties for early repayment. Usually reverts to variable rate at the end of the agreed term.

Front-end load: Charge you pay on purchase of units in unit trusts.

FSA: The Financial Services Authority which has overall responsibility for regulating financial services providers in the UK.

FSAVC: Free Standing Additional Voluntary Contributions made by employees into a money-purchase fund of their choice outside those arranged by the employer and within Inland Revenue limits – i.e. free-standing.

Full-service or advisory brokerage firms: They will charge you more in dealing commissions when they buy or sell on your behalf. They give you easier access and 'free' investment advice, and also offer services that straddle private banking and private portfolio management such as:
- Lend you money to buy shares.
- Manage your money on a 'discretionary' – that is you have no say – basis.
- Advice on trusts and tax planning.
- Design a customised private client portfolio embracing a pick and mix of securities.
- The critical factor is not cost, but quality of advice and service at such advisory firms.

Fundamentals: The essential economic criteria on which investment decisions are made.

Gearing: When a small amount of money is used initially to gain exposure, or to buy, a large underlying asset, i.e. to leverage.
- Often used in connection with borrowing only a percentage of the total value of a property (see LTV).
- Options (see derivatives) have a large element of gearing because it takes only a relatively small amount of money to buy an option to take up a large underlying asset.

George, Eddie: The Governor of the Bank of England during the historic handover of government control by New Labour in May 1997, thereby making the Bank independent. He has been an executive director of the Bank of England since 1982 and is known as 'Steady Eddie' in the City. He presides over the monetary policy committee that decides on the level of interest rates. An earlier hawkish stance on driving inflation down to, or below, the government set target of 2.5 per cent also served to keep sterling high. He appeared in spring 1999 to support Euro-sceptics over the issue of Britain joining the EMU by saying it would be an 'act of faith'. According to legend, he gained a position at the Bank of England because he was a good bridge player.

Good secondary location: Next best thing to prime property.

Government bonds: Known in the UK as gilts or gilt-edged. These are debt securities issued by the Government, and as such are normally capital safe if held to redemption, when the par value of the bonds will be paid (forget Russia). Interest is paid to investors, usually half-yearly or yearly. But long-dated gilts fluctuate in price and can lead to capital loss or profit. Income from gilts is taxable. Capital gains are tax-free within a collective fund invested in gilts and bonds. Capital gains scored from dealing directly in UK gilts is also tax-free.

Graham, Ben: Investment guru Ben Graham is the man who taught the science of 'value investing' to Warren Buffett. He wrote a classic tome, *Securities Analysis*, in 1934, in the aftermath of the Depression. By all means read it for its wit, wisdom and brilliant observation of the human factor in the stock market. Then ignore it! Do not let Graham put you off investing in great premium-rated businesses. His austere, almost actuarial analysis of shares (pertinent then) would stop you from putting your money now into brilliant businesses such as Coca-Cola, Pfizer, Merck and SmithKline Beecham. His insistence on buying only cheap 'bargain issues' at prices less than their break-up value, in order to ensure 'a margin of safety', would rule out buying shares in extraordinary businesses, albeit at premium prices.

Greenspan, Alan: Chairman of the US Federal Reserve Board August 1987, who played a pivotal role in saving the world's stock markets from a catastrophic crisis of confidence in Autumn 1998, when he cut US interest rates repeatedly by a total 0.75 per cent until calm was restored. Greenspan's remit is to devise policy to promote strong but sustainable economic growth with only low inflation in the US.

In the autumn of 1998, he also effectively devised monetary policy to manage what he termed 'dislocations abroad'. Amid increasing panic in the financial markets, Greenspan declared: 'It is just not credible that the United States can remain an oasis of prosperity unaffected by a world that is experiencing greatly increased stress.' He cut interest rates three times in quick succession to help highly indebted emerging markets service the cost of their foreign debt. Other central bankers managing large economies duly followed his lead.

Greenspan proved a remarkable stabiliser and has become a cult figure among equity investors. Critics claim his actions served to create a financial bubble on Wall Street, as investors now believe the Fed will always gallop to their rescue. Greenspan's past warnings about 'irrational exuberance' fell on deaf ears. But none can deny Greenspan is a contrarian thinker and natural sceptic with an awesome grasp of the economy. He has presided over the reorganisation of the banking system in the US and a golden era on Wall Street, and under his chairmanship the credibility and authority of the Fed has reached its highest level ever.

Gross National Product (GNP): Total value of a nation's output, based on the total value of all goods and services produced by that country, after deducting imports.

Growth share: A share in a business that is growing above the market average and also above its peer group. It often commands a higher price, reflecting higher expectations. It will pay low dividends (profits are ploughed back into the business for future growth). The amount of dividend should gradually increase as the business prospers. It may be volatile: investors do not lock in for dividends, but for capital growth. Picking out growth stocks is essentially a qualitative exercise (that is, use your judgement).

Guaranteed income bond: A fixed-term investment which, in return for a single premium, offers a guaranteed annual income. On maturity your capital is returned.

Hedge funds: Highly leveraged funds that take positions in securities or other assets they deem mispriced in the short term: their tactics include going short.

Hedging instruments: Securities designed to foil an opposite risk. To 'hedge' is to take actions to foil opposite risks.

High yield or 'junk' bonds: Corporate bonds with a credit rating of BB or lower by rating agencies, and which pay high yields to compensate for greater risk. Junk bonds are typically issued by fledgling companies, or by those in decline who cannot raise capital at cheaper rates through 'blue chip' investment grade bonds. They are a popular means of financing takeovers, and were extensively used in hostile takeover bids during the 80s. Can be highly volatile, but for risk-orientated investors who specialise in trading them, they can prove profitable. Not for the risk-averse.

Hubris: Prevalent in bull markets when principals, their advisers and investors run the danger of believing they can walk on water. It usually ends in tears. An example of hubris is when online 'day traders' in 1998/9 bought and sold virtually anything .com, without understanding how loss-making Internet businesses (as opposed to shares) could turn a profit. When, in mid-1999, the hype turned to angst, it was a case of .bomb in the share prices of some Internet companies.

Income drawdown: Drawing income from your pension fund whilst preserving your capital.

Independent financial adviser (IFA): Person qualified by virtue of having passed required examinations, and who is also authorised by regulators to give advice on every aspect of personal finance, from savings and investment to insurance, pensions and inheritance tax planning. IFA is a misnomer for one who earns commissions from providers of financial products. IFAs are increasingly charging hourly fees for advice instead of taking sales commissions. The fee trend is partly due to growing clamour about their possible conflicts of interest and pressure on providers to reduce hefty sales commissions paid to IFAs which they then add to the cost of the products sold.

Index fund or tracker fund: These funds track the general market by investing in the same shares that constitute the indices such as the FTSE-100, the S&P Futures or the DJIA. They are cheap to manage and so cost less to buy, and perform well in bull markets. They eliminate specific stock and sector risk, and merely ride the markets up or down. Some investors buy index tracker funds as 'core holdings' as they are easy to monitor. But in a sharp market decline the value of an index tracker will reflect the market's fall. They allow a natural 'weeding out' of under-performing shares that contract in value and may eventually fall out of the index. Meanwhile shares performing like top athletes will grow in price and thus gain weight in the overall index.

Inflation: The increase in the cost of goods and services. It erodes the purchasing power of money over time and as such is a hidden tax. It is measured by the UK's Retail Price Index and the US's Consumer Price Index.

Initial Public Offering (IPO) (or Offer For Sale in the UK): The debut of a company on the stock market with an initial offer to sell some or all of its shares to the general public. The relevant facts and figures about the business, its track record and prospects are published in a prospectus prior to the sale.

Inside information: Strictly illegal use of 'inside', non-public information of a price-sensitive nature, in order to deal at an unfair advantage to the rest of the market. Wall Street's infamous insider trader, Ivan Boesky, went to jail in the 80s after confessing to bribing various insiders for non-public information about certain takeover bids. He made millions out of buying shares before bids were announced (and selling them on the news).

Advisers and principals involved in a takeover bid are 'insiders' who may not deal in the securities involved in the transaction, or tell anyone else who could profit from the price-sensitive information.

Interest-only mortgage: A property loan on which no capital is paid monthly, but only interest, and the entire outstanding debt is repaid at term.

ISA (Individual Savings Accounts): Tax shelters for UK residents, aged at least 18 years, started on 6 April 1999 (replacing PEPs) to promote investment outside pension plans. Tax-free status guaranteed until 2009. Can invest tax-free in shares and bonds, life insurance and cash, via ISAs, subject to limits. The maximum allowed in 1999/2000 is £7,000, and £5,000 thereafter. The Mini-ISA allows you to pick and mix managers and put in up to £3,000 in cash, a like amount in shares/bonds and £1,000 in insurance in 1999/2000; but £1,000 in cash, £1,000 in insurance and £3,000 in shares thereafter. The cocktail in a Mini-ISA will erode the amount you can put into shares tax-free. The Maxi-ISA allows the maximum to go into shares and/or bonds. The Maxi-ISA will make you maxi-profits over the long term (at mini-complication). Income from shares within the ISA will be eroded by (a further) 10 per cent by changes in ACT from April 2004.

Low-start mortgage: This gives you a 'holiday' with low costs, in a repayment mortgage during the first few years. The capital component in the normal monthly mortgage repayment is deferred. But beware a sense of false security as the unpaid capital remains outstanding, pushing up the cost of your repayments later.

LTV: The loan-to-value ratio expressed, as a percentage, in a property loan.

Management fee: The fee charged by a fund manager of a private portfolio or collective fund such as a unit trust or investment trust for the services of his or her firm. The management fee is usually based on the value of the assets under management. The fee is not the primary consideration when choosing a fund manager – performance is. But the fees charged are a consideration as they will erode growth of the fund over time.

Money market funds: Virtually cash funds: the securities in which the fund is invested will typically be short term government bonds and cash equivalents with little or no risk of capital loss, and they do provide an income.

Net asset value (NAV): The market value of a share in a unit trust or any open-ended fund. In the case of a closed-ended fund, it is the value of the underlying assets.

Net worth: The total amount an individual or a company is worth after calculating the market value of all assets and deducting all liabilities, including outstanding debts.

Online trading: Buying and selling over the Internet. If day trading, it might be on a rolling settlement of T + 5 working days in the UK.

The main advantage is you can deal for far less and on virtually the same footing, in terms of instant access and information, as a professional investor. Use only a leading online broker. You can get quality company and industry research, and daily market commentary as well as good execution. But beware: you could so easily fall into the trap of trying to beat the market with frequent trading, which, at whatever discounted rate, is not normally a profitable exercise. You would pay stamp duty when you buy. The temptation to trade/gamble beyond your means online is very great. A wise investor, particularly one that may be rattled by the market, slows down, asks questions and obtains written information before reaching a rational investment decision. That decision-making process is speeded up online, so you are in greater danger of making investment mistakes.

The risks are even greater if you are not sure what shares to buy. As a beginner, you ought to start investing via an advisory broker until you have the knowledge and confidence to deal online. Moreover, cyberspace is full of con men and fraudsters using new technology to play old tricks to cheat naïve investors with promises of quick profits. Before you buy shares online, make sure you know and understand how the company in which you are investing makes money. Never rely solely on what you read online to make an investment decision.

Don't trade online unless you are confident in your investment knowledge.

Open-ended investment companies (oeics): A hybrid between unit trusts and investment trusts. The legal structure is that of a limited company (the roles of a unit trust manager and trustee are played by the authorised corporate director and an independent depository). You buy shares in the oeic rather than units as in a unit trust. There is no bid/offer spread, but a single price to which an initial sales charge is added. Shares are priced on the basis of net asset value.

Open-ended fund: A fund whose shares trade at net asset value (NAV) of their investments – plus or minus charges.

Penny stock: Traditionally these shares were literally priced for a few pennies and had tiny capitalisations. In the UK the Alternative

Investment Market (AIM) has allowed fledgling companies, which cannot meet the criteria for a full listing, to trade. They can be priced at much more than a few pence, but remain small capitalisation stocks. They are highly volatile, as trading is thin. The 'spreads' in prices quoted to buyers and sellers as opposed to a seller are inordinately large, and substantially reduce the value you realise when you sell, and increase costs when you buy.

PEP (Personal Equity Plan): A tax shelter for shares and bonds, introduced in 1987 by the Conservatives and abolished by New Labour who replaced it with the ISA in 1999/2000. Only for UK residents aged over 18 years who could invest up to £9,000 per tax year. Existing PEPs are still potent. Led to explosive growth in financial services in the UK (notably in unit trusts). Flexible and tax-free, but dividend income within existing PEPs will be eroded by ACT changes from 2004. Great alternatives to personal pensions and more generous than the ISA.

Pooled pension investment (PPI): Initially dubbed 'Lisa' by the media (long term individual savings account), this is planned to star in New Labour's constellation of alternative investment vehicles to conventional personal pensions contracts offered by life insurers. Each investor would own his or her own individual account within a pooled fund. That should allow greater flexibility to move jobs and to take the savings account with you or to switch from one fund manager to another without incurring heavy penalties. Yet to become a reality.

Portfolio: A collection of financial holdings and other assets owned by a private investor, institution or trust. Balanced portfolios are a mix of fixed-interest and equity investments. Growth-orientated portfolios can be 80 per cent shares and 20 per cent fixed-interest or 100 per cent shares. An all equity portfolio will be 100 per cent invested in shares. Fixed-interest portfolios invest only in gilts and bonds and are designed to produce income.

Positive yield gap: The excess of return between one class of asset and another.

Premium: The sum of money paid at pre-agreed intervals to an insurance company in return for cover against potential future events such as illness, death, theft or car accidents. Insurance companies invest your premiums for profit which should in turn reduce them. Outside insurance, it is the price paid over par value. It can also be the price paid for an option.

Price earnings ratio: The ratio between a company's share price and the net earnings attributable to that class of share. It gives you an idea of how much you are paying for expectations of that company's earnings growth. The higher the p/e ratio, the more you are paying for those expectations.

Prime location: The best possible location.

Registered representative: An employee of a Stock Exchange member broker or authorised dealer, who is qualified and authorised to act as an adviser and/or fund manager for clients. Must pass a basic examination and is subject to compliance by an authorised firm.

Repayment mortgage: A property loan whereby interest and capital are paid off in equal monthly instalments.

Reversion: The end of a lease (notice to stay or leave with future rent an open negotiation).

Review: A regular scheduled change in the rent (invariably upwards) to market rental value.

Rights issue: Shares are offered to existing shareholders (who have rights) often at a discount to raise funds for the company. A prospectus is published setting out the financial effect of and the reasons for a rights issue. Rights not taken up can be sold for a profit by the shareholder.

Risk-averse: The characteristic of an investor who cannot afford, or psychologically sustain, risk. It is a fallacy that investors can avoid inordinate risk of capital loss by investing only in 'safer' securities, while those who assume greater risk can also expect a higher return.

Systemic risk is inherent in securities markets and prevalent twenty-four hours a day.

Specific sector and stock risk can be reduced – with the right choices. Nothing is certain in investment but use of common sense does reduce the risk of mistakes.

Scheiber, Anne: A little-known spinster who stunned financial circles when she died, aged 101, with a fortune of $22 million in stocks and bonds, amassed over fifty years from an original nest egg of $25,000. Her former broker, William Fay, now retired from Merrill Lynch, says money meant little to her, although she would check into his Madison Avenue office three times a week to ask how much she was worth – the score that gave meaning to her passion.

She retired from the IRS (America's Inland Revenue), aged 50, in 1944, and over the next fifty years, even during the severe and protracted bear market during the 70s, Scheiber persistently and patiently invested and re-invested her dividends and profits in blue chip shares and tax-free municipal bonds. She liked businesses with big franchises – Pepsi-Cola, Schering Plough and Bristol Myers were among her core holdings.

Scheiber was a product of her time, her family having been hit by the Depression. She loved going to the movies in the 30s and 40s and finally turned that interest into investment in the large Hollywood studios, which are now multi-media combines. No-one could persuade her to spend money: she was simply not interested in consuming, just in investing. She would base her 'research' on reading the *Wall Street Journal* and the *New York Times*, and whatever research Merrill Lynch gave her to update her on her shares.

She loved to go to the annual meetings of companies in which she owned shares. She enjoyed the freebies, and occasionally would ask pertinent questions. Her simple strategy required great discipline, which she had in abundance. She left the bulk of her fortune to the Yeshiva University's Stern College for Women in New York, so that young, under-privileged Jewish women could get a scholarship, and combat the discrimination she felt she had encountered during her twenty-three years at the IRS.

Scrip issue: Known as a 'bonus issue' or in the US, a 'stock split'. The purpose is to increase liquidity in the market by issuing free shares (in proportion to your existing holding) and thus reducing share prices. Nothing extra is given away, but scrip issues make existing investors feel good and make shares more marketable. If, for example, a 300-pence share is split three-for-one the price is reduced to 100 pence and existing shareholders get two new shares for every one held. Earnings per share and dividend per share adjust proportionately, but ratios remain the same, and so does the market capitalisation.

Settlement: A securities transaction once agreed must be settled, a process that involves transfer of ownership of stocks from seller to buyer and then transfer of cash from buyer to seller. 'Trade confirmation' and settlement should be immediate, but in the UK settlement normally takes five working days after the trade – expressed as T + 5. It takes only three days in the US.

Share buy-backs: A company buys back its own shares, thus reducing the pool of shares outstanding. Common in the US where the likes of IBM and General Motors have launched billion-dollar share buy-backs, boosting confidence and their share prices in so doing.

Share certificate: The document certifying the registered holder (owner) of a company's shares. The certificate is issued at the time of purchase and shows the number of shares owned, the type of shares purchased and their par value. The name and address of the registered holder will be on the certificate and should the shares be subsequently sold, the exact name and spelling of it should be used in execution. It should be kept safe and its number and the reference noted in a ledger in case it is lost. A transfer form must be completed if the shares change hands – even within a family. If you sell fewer shares than you own, send the broker your certificate for the lot, and a new certificate for the balance will be returned to you. This procedure is fast being replaced by paperless transactions thanks to technology.

Single-premium bonds: Investments in life companies' managed funds or unit-linked funds. Often recommended as a tax shelter but they are tax-paid, not tax-free.

Soros, George: The billionaire financier who became notorious in September 1992 when he made almost $1 billion profit betting against the pound within the European Exchange Rate Mechanism (ERM). Soros' hedge fund, Quantum, is legendary among investors who got in during its earliest years. A $1,000 investment in Quantum in 1969 would have been worth some $3 million at the end of 1998. Soros stalks world markets seeking out often temporary dislocations from which to profit. He is certainly not in the buy-and-hold camp, nor indeed an inspired stock picker. He looks at the big picture, spots what is going wrong and places his bets accordingly.

Soros epitomises the power of global market forces over governments. He defends the activities of hedge funds as forcing a discipline on central banks. He has advocated controls and limits to the free movement of capital because, he says, otherwise our system could collapse from its inherent flaws. He talks of a 'wrecking ball' effect during crises in world markets. His book *The Crisis of Global Markets*, based on the Asian crisis, was published in autumn 1998.

A year before, amid financial crisis and forest fires, Malaysia's Prime Minister Mahathir Mohamad attacked 'immoral' financial speculators and called Soros a 'moron'. Soros countered that Dr Mahathir was 'a menace to his country'.

Born in Budapest in 1930 into a middle-class Jewish family, he experienced both Nazism and Communism before emigrating to Britain in 1947. At the London School of Economics, Soros was influenced by Karl Popper, philosopher and author of *The Open Society and its Enemies*, a work that inspired his investment philosophy 'Reflexivity', and later helped to shape Soros' philanthropic activities.

Split-capital investment trusts: Investment trusts which terminate at a fixed-term and typically with income shares, capital shares and zero-dividend preference shares. These different classes of shares give you rights to different parts of the income and capital gains generated by the investments trust's share portfolio.

- **Income shares.** There are several types. The traditional income share gives a right to all of the dividend income from the share portfolio and a fixed redemption price (usually equal to issue price) is repaid at term. Some income shares are annuity-like in that they pay high income but are deliberately designed to give rise to capital losses at redemption – useful for investors with taxable capital gains in their portfolios against which to offset losses.

The ordinary income share is found in trusts in combination with zero-dividend preference shares and entitle you to all the income and surplus capital after the holders of the zeros have been paid off.

- **Capital shares** are potentially the most rewarding component of a split-capital trust. Shareholders are entitled to the capital remaining after all other classes of share and borrowings have been repaid. They receive no income, but the capital gain – although not guaranteed – can be great because of the gearing effect of the other classes of shares.
- **Zero-dividend preference shares (zeros)** are found in a split capital investment trust. They pay a fixed sum at a fixed redemption date, synchronised with the end of the life of the trust (typically no more than ten years). Zeros are investment heroes for the risk-averse, for although they pay no income, they have preferential rights over the share-out of capital at the end of a trust's life. Profits from zeros are taxed as capital gains not income, so are attractive if you are not using your annual capital gains tax exemption (£7,100 in 1999/2000). Zeros rise in value according to a pre-determined compound annual growth rate but also reflecting prevailing interest rates. In theory, in the event of a major failure, a trust could not meet the full redemption value of zeros – but that risk is small, particularly if you invest in well managed, high quality trusts.

Stagflation: Inflation without corresponding increase in output, demand and employment.

Stamp duty: Tax due when you buy shares or property, based on its value. At 1999/2000 it is:
- 0.5 per cent on shares.
- nil on properties worth up to £60,000.
- 1 per cent on properties worth £60,001 – £250,000.
- 2.5 per cent on properties worth £250,001 – £500,000.
- 3.5 per cent on properties worth over £500,000.

Standard & Poor's Composite Index of 500 stocks (S&P 500): Broad-based measurement of changes in US stock market conditions based on the average performance of 500 widely held shares. The index tracks industrial, transportation, financial and utility shares. Composed mostly of blue chips listed on the NY Stock Exchange.

Standard & Poor's Corporation: A securities rating agency, also publishes several other important indices, including the S&P MidCap 400 and the S&P 600 SmallCap Index.

Stock Exchange: An organised institution wherein stocks and bonds are traded in a market by the members who act both as brokers and principal traders dealing in their own accounts.

Tax-efficient investment: Can add up to substantial 'tax-free' income if you use to the limit all the various income tax and capital gains tax allowances each tax year and also take advantage of tax sheltered savings schemes available. Tax efficiency should not drive investment decisions but it is a major consideration.
- Individual personal allowance is not taxable (£4,335 in 1999/2000).
- Each person has a capital gains tax exemption (£7,100 in 1999/2000).
- Income from National Savings certificates is tax-free but capital is locked in for five years.
- Contributions to a pension fund enjoy tax relief at your highest marginal rate.
- Income from (mature) TESSAs (taken out before 6 April 1999) is tax-free.
- ISA (see above).
- Existing, pre-1999 PEPs are similarly tax-sheltered, and can be retained.
- Gilts (UK Government bonds) are free of capital gains.
- Sale of your principal residence is normally free of capital gains tax.
- Inheritance tax (IHT) is not charged on estates worth up to £231,000 (1999/2000).
- IHT can be mitigated by transferring assets in excess of £231,000 to beneficiaries during your lifetime and hopefully surviving seven years – after which it is tax-free. You can also take out a seven year term insurance to cover the potential IHT liability on your transfers in the event of untimely death.

Term life assurance: A life insurance policy that gives you cover for a specified amount over an agreed term. If you die within that term, your beneficiaries receive the specified amount. But if you survive, the insurance expires at the 'deadline' with no cash value. It is the most cost-effective way to insure against untimely death during a period of time. It is also used to mitigate against IHT when gifting assets.

TESSA: Tax-efficient special savings accounts. Introduced in 1990. Abolished on 6 April 1999, but existing plans remain valid. Tax-free cash savings account for investors aged eighteen and over. A total of £9,000 could be deposited over five years, with a maximum of £3,000 in the first year, £1,800 for each of the next three years and £600 in the final (fifth) year. Provided the capital remained locked in for five years, all the interest was tax-free.

Tietmeyer, Hans: President of the Bundesbank until spring 1999. Played a pivotal role in the management of the German economy in the run up to the launch of the Euro in January 1999.

Top line: American business speak for 'sales'.

Total return: The annual return on an investment which adds the dividends earned, or interest earned, plus any appreciation in the value of the share or bond.

Unit trusts: Or mutual funds in the US, are 'open-ended' funds and their price, as quoted in the daily newspaper, reflects the value of their underlying assets divided by the number of units, in the fund (sometimes less a redemption charge).

US Treasuries: Are bonds issued by the US Federal Government and are considered a safe haven as the US Government can be expected to repay its debt in full. There are three types of Treasuries:
- Bills are loans for one year or less. Minimum purchase is normally $5,000.
- Notes are loans for 1 to 10 years. Minimum purchase is $1,000.
- Bonds are loans for 10 to 30 years. Minimum purchase is $1,000.

Value Investing: Is contrarian as you buy shares that are poorly regarded by the market (but which you believe are undervalued).

They often have a low ratio of price to book value, low price earnings ratio, or a high dividend yield. But as Warren Buffett says, the distinction between value investing and its opposite, growth investing, is 'fuzzy thinking' because the two approaches are 'joined at the hip'. He argues: 'What is "investing" if it is not seeking value at least sufficient to justify the amount paid?' He concludes that the characteristics of value shares – even if they appear in combination – are no guarantee that an investor is indeed buying something for what it is worth. Correspondingly, opposite characteristics – a high ratio of price to book value, a high price earnings ratio, and a low dividend (characteristics of so-called growth shares) are 'in no way inconsistent with a "value" purchase'. He concludes: 'the very term "value investing" is redundant'.

Variable annuity: Big in the US and coming to Europe, this is an annuity that depends on stock market performance rather than interest rates. It is a life insurance product that includes a link to an equity portfolio. Income can fluctuate. Riskier than a plain vanilla annuity, which is invested in fixed-income securities. Not predictable, while a fixed annuity is. As with most annuities, your capital is exchanged for income.

Variable-rate mortgage: A mortgage loan whose rate of interest fluctuates according to changes in base rate. The opposite of a fixed-rate mortgage. Can be advantageous during periods of sharp falls in interest rates. If interest rates are low, a fixed-rate mortgage can be better, as rates may rise again.

Volatility: The change in market value of a security. Online dealing has increased market volatility by enabling private investors to buy and sell shares and bonds rather like foreign exchange dealers trade currencies. It is unsettling emotionally, like riding a roller-coaster of fear and greed. Instant communications and linkage of world markets has increased volatility short term. Investors demand higher returns from volatile funds and shares to compensate for risk. Wise investors sit tight on good shares during turbulence – missing out on the best months can decimate your performance long term.

For example, investment bankers CSFB claim, in their 1999 Equity-Gilt Study, that £100 invested in an equity fund in 1918 would have been worth just over £1 million at the end of 1998.[5] Had an investor (miraculously) ducked out of the ten *worst* performing months during that period, his £100 would have been worth £6,464,554. But even more striking (and costly) is the fact that had the investor been out of the stock market during the *best* ten months in that 80-year period, his original £100 would be worth only £159,854.

Wall Street: Traditionally the financial district of New York, because the New York Stock Exchange is at 11 Wall Street. More than an address in downtown Manhattan, Wall Street is a generic name for a whole industry. New York is the world's most influential financial centre, followed by London and Tokyo. California is the centre of Silicon Valley, the heartland of the technology companies that account for the lion's share of the capital spending of US business. IT and deregulation allow private investors in western economies to key into stock markets beyond their own borders to buy foreign shares and bonds electronically.

Warrants: Options issued by a company which give holders the right to buy ordinary shares at a predetermined price – called strike price or exercise price – within a set term. If the warrant has not been exercised within the term, it expires worthless. Warrant holders cannot vote. Warrants do not pay dividends.

Whole of life insurance: A type of life insurance that pays a benefit at death and also builds up a cash value over time. Should not be viewed as a surrogate investment/savings vehicle. The cost of life cover (including sales commissions) is higher than with term assurance. The investment returns are relatively low. Often sold more with the interests of the advisers (commission salesmen) in mind than that of the savers. Can be used for inheritance tax planning.

With-profits: An insurance investment that provides returns to investors by means of annual bonuses and a terminal bonus, payable at maturity. The bonuses are calculated to reflect the investment returns generated by the insurance company, and those returns are smoothed over a business cycle.

---

[5] Assuming all dividends were reinvested gross.

With-profits bonds: A single premium bond investment in a with-profits fund of a life insurance company (see single-premium bonds).

With-profits life insurance: A life insurance plan that may be whole of life, or have a limited term where the investment return is related to a with-profits investment vehicle (see previous page).

Yield: The return, by way of share dividend, rental received or interest derived, on bonds or gilts. Expressed as a percentage of the market price, or of the capital value in the case of property.

Zero-coupon bond: A bond sold at a deep discount because it pays no interest as do conventional bonds, but when it is redeemed at an agreed maturity date it will repay a fixed price.

Index